Faith Development

Building Faith One Child at a Time

Becky Schuricht Peters

Edited by Thomas J. Doyle
and Arnold E. Schmidt

Gary Bertels and Marian Baden,
Consultants

CPH®
Concordia Publishing House

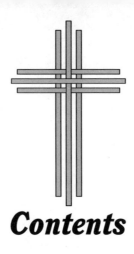

Contents

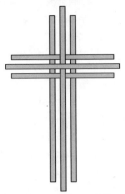

Publisher's Preface

Why publish a book about faith development? Doesn't faith grow by the power of the Holy Spirit? And doesn't the Spirit work through God's Word, Baptism, and the Lord's Supper? Then why cloud the issue with psychological theories?

Faith does grow only by the power of the Holy Spirit. Nothing we do can cause faith to begin or grow in someone's life. Only God can do that. Everything in this volume must rest on that basic principle.

Faith development is clearly God's work, not ours. But God gave us the task of sharing the faith, and He encourages us to be more shrewd than the world in sharing the treasures of the Gospel (Luke 16:8). Even as the proper use of Law and Gospel involves rightly dividing their application, so Christian education involves some assessment of classes and students. Research on faith development helps us give milk and solid food, each at the proper time (Hebrews 5:12). This information is another resource, a tool we use to help prepare, plan, and implement good teaching methods. As God gives information, so we rejoice in the opportunities to use it as a blessing of His hand.

A caution is in order, too. Faith development language and strategies are not designed for judging whether or not faith exists in the human heart; only God knows its contents. Neither should we use this information as a template for evaluating "good" faith or "weak" faith. Saving, active, vibrant faith is God's gift, not a level of human development or application. We are saved by grace through faith in Christ Jesus (Ephesians 2:8).

This book addresses the human development model and gives

teachers additional strategies for designing and developing age-appropriate lesson plans that properly match the level and abilities of the students. We here add form, substance, and helpful direction to the teacher who wants in every opportunity to *be prepared to give an answer to everyone who asks you to give the reason for the hope that you have* (1 Peter 3:15).

We find examples in Jesus' ministry that demonstrate that the context in which God's message is shared is significant; Jesus' words and actions fit the context. He emphasized the importance and faith of young children when adults brought these children to Him (Matthew 19:13–15; Mark 10:13–16; Luke 18:15–17). He taught about the cause of suffering when He saw a man blind from birth (John 9:1–7).

So today we also consider the context of a learning situation as we design that experience. That context includes factors such as methods, materials, and the various developmental stages of learners. When learners cannot comprehend complex, abstract truths, we stick to simple, concrete messages. When learners are challenging authority, we attempt to provide an appropriate environment—one that allows them to challenge, but continues to demonstrate God's love and power through words and actions.

Thus, in Christian education we *always* rely on God to create and strengthen faith. As you provide Christian education opportunities that consider the context of the experiences, pray that God may mightily use you to proclaim His Word. May He bless you as you embark on this journey with us.

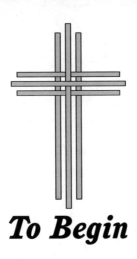

To Begin

Picture a block, like a child's building block. It's sitting on a table in front of you. You didn't put it there. Staring at it straight on, you can see the letter on the top and the letter on the face directly in front of you. With a slight lean to the left and the right you can view two more sides. Yet two sides remain hidden. If you were to walk around the table, one more side would be revealed. But the bottom remains obscured. Without the ability to pick it up (or a glass table), you will never know what's on the bottom of the block; the total picture of the block is incomplete.

Perhaps this explains our human view of faith and how it grows. Countless studies have been made in a variety of related fields. Experts have generated theories of cognitive learning, social growth, emotional maturation, and moral development that affect our understanding of faith. But just like the sides of a block, theory alone does not provide a complete picture. To grasp the reality of a three-dimensional block, more than one side must be visible.

Faith is a gift of God through the workings of the Holy Spirit. The theories of Piaget, Kohlberg, Erikson, Westerhoff, and Fowler all attempt to lend to our understanding of faith. The Scriptures are filled with stories of the faithful, and every Christian can tell how he or she has experienced faith. But the complete picture of the block of faith remains a mystery in spite of all of our human efforts to get a clear picture. As St. Paul lamented, *Now we see but a poor reflection as in a mirror; then we shall see face to face. Now I know in part; then I shall know fully, even as I am fully known* (1 Corinthians 13:12).

7

In examining the block of faith we will look at what God tells us in His holy, inspired Word. We will also consider individual stories of faith both from the modern world and those stories of the heros and heroines of faith as found in the Scriptures. We'll explore what we think faith to be, what experts in a variety of fields have theorized, how their theories apply to faith development, and practical application of strategies that can assist in the growth of our students' faith. Perhaps most crucial to our understanding of faith is admitting that our grasp of this area of life is less than perfect. We are and always will be lacking in complete knowledge and emotion of the full view of faith, at least while yet in this world.

I invite you to think of this book as a workbook or journal. As I have struggled with the writing of it, I have spent much time contemplating my faith—not so much the content, but rather its structure and form. I realize that the journey has been an interesting one but one that I have sometimes taken for granted or even to which I've been oblivious. In various crises my faith development has regressed as well as grown. Those times of growth have often been painful, but necessary, as I struggle toward spiritual maturity.

As you read through the chapters, please take the time to examine your own faith life. Perhaps some readers will find it most useful to study in a group setting. Discussing the features of faith with others can broaden your horizons. Verbalizing your own faith and the route you have taken to this point in your life can itself be a growth experience.

This book isn't, and doesn't pretend to be, the final word on faith or spiritual maturity, but I pray that it is a worthwhile guide as you seek to better understand where you have been, where you are headed, and where you hope to lead others.

Becky Peters

What Is Faith?

You're a teacher. Not only are you a Christian teacher, but you teach in a Christian setting and you're expected to nurture your students in the Christian faith. In fact, faith is what your class is all about. Whether it's a Sunday school class, midweek school, vacation Bible school, a day school religion class, or confirmation class, some people would define your job as "teaching the faith."

Most Christians would agree that "teaching the faith" is more than just telling Bible stories and expecting students to memorize Bible verses. Teachers want students not only to know the story but to make it their own story by applying it to their lives. A teacher desires to guide students to see that the same God who rescued the Hebrews from the hands of the Egyptians is the God who rescues them from sin and the power of the devil. More than just to inform students how Jesus made a difference in the life of the man born blind, teachers want to help students experience how Jesus can open their eyes to the potential God has planned for them. A teacher aims not just to teach how the early Christian community of believers lived their faith in troubled times but to enable the students to participate in that faith community even in the midst of disaster.

How do we do that? How does faith start? How does faith grow? How does one move from a baptized baby to a confirmand to a committed adult Christian who strives to live his or her faith no matter what the situation? What influence or control does the individual Christian have in this matter? What is the role of Christian education?

So many questions need to be answered. This book attempts to assist you in finding the solutions.

A QUESTION OF FAITH

What is faith? How do you define it? It's one thing to explain the content of your faith—"I believe in God, the Father Almighty, maker of heaven and earth. And in Jesus Christ, his only Son ..."— but it's another to explain accurately what faith is, especially if you are referring to faith as it might apply to any of the world's major religions. Right now, before you read another word, grab a pencil or pen, and jot down your definition of faith.

Some people might explain faith as knowing something. Others might say that faith is believing to be true something that can't be proved. Yet limiting faith to just knowing or believing a body of knowledge, such as the Apostles' Creed, is incomplete. However, if we examine the history of the word *creed,* some interesting information is revealed.

The Latin word *credo* is usually translated into English as "I believe." The word *credo* comes from two different words, one meaning "heart" and the other meaning "put, place, set, or give." Thus the word *creed* implies more than just a belief about a set of facts. It reveals where we put our hearts or to what we give our hearts. Many other languages reveal a similar background when examining their words for faith. Through the centuries, especially in our scientific age, the word has been watered down to refer to merely accepting something as true ("I have faith that this detergent will get out grass stains") or putting our confidence in someone ("I have faith that my pastor will visit me in the hospital").

Dr. James Fowler, a researcher who has devoted his career to examining the concept of faith, explains faith as the way one gives meaning to life. More than just a way of knowing something, it is the lens through which we view our world. According to Fowler's theories, faith colors our entire perception of life. What one has faith in is what one is committed to. What one is committed to is evidenced by where one has placed one's heart. There you will find loyalty, trust, and love.

WHAT IS FAITH?

Now do a little self-examination. (This could be painful.) Where do you put your heart? What has a high time priority? What are those things you wouldn't miss for the world?

Ouch! If you're like me, I look at my list and cringe. I make excuses. "I need some relaxation time—some downtime. God wants me to take care of myself. My (fill in the blank) is a gift from God, and I want to be a good steward." All these things may be true, but it still comes down to priorities. Do you make God a priority in your life? How often do you find yourself taking God and your faith for granted? How easy is it for you to forget that your relationship with God takes effort just like any other relationship? Thank God that He forgives us through Jesus when we put that relationship on the "back burner."

I am in a faith relationship with God, and I've known it for a long time. But it's not easy to explain exactly what that means to me. I believe in a God who loved me so much that He sent His only Son whom He dearly loved to die a horrible death on the cross so that I may be His own on earth and live eternally with Him in heaven. Even though my heart sometimes gets sidetracked by meaningless diversions, I know with all of my being that God loves and cares for me. I know this "knowledge" at a deeper level than I know any other fact I might be able to prove in a scientific manner. This "knowledge" forms a core part of my being; indeed, I can't perceive me being "me" without it.

I base this knowledge on a trust unlike any other trust relationship in my life. This trust is difficult to explain. Some would say it doesn't make sense, especially in the eyes of the world. My solid trust does not depend on what I know in my brain but rather on what seems to be rooted in my heart. The roots of this trust are firmly entrenched and reach deep into my being. It is not invincible, but it is resistant to disease. Most of all, I do not base my trust on anything I have done. It seems to thrive in spite of myself.

THE CONCEPT OF TRUST

When some people look at trust, they see it as something a person does, something that is self-initiated, something I *do*. There are some people I trust; however, that trust usually depends on their past performance. I trust my husband to be faithful to our marriage vows. He has never given me reason to doubt him. But I suppose that could change if circumstances were to change. For 20-some years I trusted my father to be all that God wanted him to be as a husband and father. He had always modeled the Christian life to his family, his neighbors, and his congregation. But that changed when he strayed from his marriage vows. Then I no longer trusted him.

When looking at trust this way, the concept of trust as a synonym for faith is weak. I choose to trust my husband, and that trust is based on both of our behaviors. My trust could easily break down if I happen to misinterpret events even if he has done nothing to break the trust. I can choose to trust or mistrust someone based on the way I choose to interpret events.

If one defines faith as trust, we must approach it differently. The Bible tells me that faith comes through the Holy Spirit; I can do nothing to initiate it on my own. Yet investigate the word *faith* and you'll find that it comes from the Latin word *fidere,* which means "to trust." Where is the source of this trust?

Many people have tried to discover precisely where faith begins. There are several theories. Two key components of faith dominate these debates: knowledge and trust.

Some people believe that faith begins with knowledge. In the Christian faith, this knowledge comes from hearing the Word of God. In His Word we discover all that God has done for us. He created and preserves us. He sent His Son to atone for our sins and promises eternal life to all believers. Through the Gospel (this Good News) the Holy Spirit creates and strengthens faith in the Christian's heart. The individual could choose to reject this work of the Spirit, but when the Spirit is not rejected, faith grows. The Christian hears God's Word and trusts it through the power of the Holy Spirit.

Other people reverse the components of faith. They believe that trust is the beginning of faith. God the Holy Spirit plants the trust in the heart of the believer. Once that trust is acknowledged, the believer seeks more understanding of this reliance and strives to build the base of knowledge. Faith can begin at any age; however, some think the idea of faith beginning with trust can best be explained by looking at a young child. An infant experiences trust when her parents consistently provide for her needs. Trust appears to develop before knowledge. Consider also a person who has just fallen in love. In love at first sight, young people fall in "love" without knowing the object of their desire very well. But an important part of being in love anticipates discovering all there is to know about the beloved. The same might be said of the new believer in Christ. Trust can exist without a broad base of biblical knowledge. Trust results in an intense search to deepen the relationship by getting to know more about God the Lover.

HEAD VS. HEART?

We often talk about head knowledge versus heart knowledge. The idea of trust (heart) versus knowledge (head) seems to fit right into the debate. Heart knowledge reveals the relationship we have with our God. Head knowledge reflects the content of our faith. Which is more important?

All people are an interesting blend of intellect and emotion in an infinite variety of combinations. Some people operate on their feelings while others base decisions on logical explanations. Although most individuals have a dominant way of looking at the world, a few are so strong on one side or the other that they never consider the weaker area. When the combination of intellect and emotion is totally one-sided, the effect can adversely impact the person's life.

People perceive a person with all intellect and no emotion as cold and uncaring. His life is based on reason, and if reason can't answer the question, he discards the question. Apply this to the spiritual side of life. A person might have extensive knowledge of the Bible and the attributes of God and yet have no commitment to the Christian faith. This type of knowledge alone does not lead to salvation.

All emotion and no knowledge, on the other hand, leads to a shallow understanding of God and His plan for people. When challenged, this person's faith has little to fall back on. Just as the seed sown on the path was trampled and eaten by birds, a lack of head knowledge provides no anchor for the storms of life. See Luke 8:5–15.

Teachers of the Christian faith face the challenge of feeding the head as well as the heart in a nutritious blend of servings. Is one more important than the other? As you can see, it is not easy to pinpoint faith and how it grows. I am led to what I know best: how God has worked in my life. Perhaps looking at my story of faith will help my understanding of it.

MY STORY OF FAITH

My father was raised in the Lutheran church. His side of the family goes back to the Lutherans who left Germany in the 1850s to pursue a new life in the United States. He met my mother at a youth group function; she was attending with a friend. They were married in Zion Lutheran Church. Their first two children were baptized there. Child number three (me) was no different. At three weeks of age, I was baptized in the church that my grandfather had helped establish.

God was very much a part of my early years. Although my family moved to a newer suburb with Lutheran churches close by, we faithfully attended Zion every week. Our routine always included mealtime and bedtime prayers. We were expected to live by the Golden Rule and the Ten Commandments. My father taught a Bible class and sang in the church choir.

At the age of three, I started Sunday school, which was a fixture of my life through high school. As an elementary student, I knew that some people were not Christian, but to me, those people lived strange lives in distant countries. I wasn't sure about Catholics and worried about the salvation of my Catholic neighbor. Our closest family friends were members of the same congregation. In other words, religion and faith were part of my life just as much as brushing my teeth before I went to bed.

My best friend and I lived about seven miles apart, but we saw each other every day except Saturday. Our families were members of the same church. My dad had known her parents since they were in high school. Some Saturday evenings we were together because our parents played cards once a month. I spent a lot of nights at her house and she at mine. Her parents became my "second parents." Not only would they reprimand me if I needed it, I knew they cared for me. They talked to me and listened as few adults listen to children. I was always comfortable at their home, and I always felt welcome. With their own six children and friends of their children, their house was always a bustling, fun place to be. The best part about it was that my "second parents" shared family devotions, family prayers, and comfortably talked about God in their daily life with anyone and everyone who might be visiting.

I attended a Christian day school for eight years. Religion class was a daily part of the schedule, except on Wednesdays when we went to chapel. Sometimes the pastor preached; sometimes we watched "Parables from Nature." The students in my class all attended church with me on Sunday mornings, even though not all were as regular in attendance as my family was.

Although I think I can name every teacher I had in those eight years of elementary school, one stands out. She was only with us for the first semester of my sixth-grade year. As a first-year teacher she drove some of the parents crazy because she liked to throw capital *E*s into the middle of words. But it wasn't her nonconformity to the rules of handwriting that makes me remember her. She cared about us and showed it continually. Once when I was the one ostracized from the group and devastated, she put her arms around me, held me, and simply said, "It will get better." She made me feel loved instead of feeling like an outcast. I'll never forget her.

In eighth grade I attended confirmation class taught by our pastor four mornings a week. The class requirements included much memorization, some of which would be recited before the congregation on Pentecost. The pastor was stern and strict in his expectations, but he also revealed a friendly side. My strongest memory from our confirmation service is that my classmates looked to me to start them out in all of our memorized responses. Somewhat panicked about this, I grabbed a pen right before church started and wrote the various beginning words to our answers on my hands. Feeling somewhat confident but still nervous, we stood as a group to answer the pastor's questions. I took a deep breath and looked down as my friends looked at me. I was horrified to discover how easily ink smears on sweaty hands. Somehow we all got through those responses.

The summer after ninth grade marked a turning point in my life. In the previous year we had transferred to a closer congregation due to my father working more Saturday nights and not getting home early enough to make the seven-mile drive to Zion. Being quiet and shy and unskilled at saying no, I was elected to office in the youth group as the Christian Growth Chairman. One Sunday our pastor announced that the congregation would be sending the Christian Growth Chairman to LSV (Lutheran Service Volunteer), a camp program sponsored by the Missouri Synod. His first question was, "Who's Christian Growth Chairman?"

Since the church was paying for the trip, my parents sent me off to the mountains. I was exposed to a week of intense Bible study and fellowship that added "heart knowledge" to my solid base of "head knowledge." For the first time in my life, I felt and consciously believed that faith was more than what I believed about God. I had always "known" I was a Christian, but it was a type of knowing similar to knowing I was female. That same summer I attended a district youth gathering. Suddenly, I had the intense desire to be part of God's family, and I wanted to commit my life to that purpose.

After that I became actively involved in many different youth activities in my own church and at the district level. I felt very strongly that God was guiding my life. Although still quiet and shy at my large public high school, with my church friends I was a leader. I was involved with a group of teens that led retreats for other congregations. I was president of the youth groups in my zone. I wrote Bible studies and read theology books. I could boldly proclaim to strangers that I was a committed Christian and that nothing would ever separate me from God's love. The popular boys in high school never asked me out, but in my yearbook they wrote that they respected me and the way I lived what I believed. I decided that I could live with that.

After high school graduation my closest friends left for college. I daily drove to the local community college. But life had changed. I was still involved with youth activities at church, but I felt that it was time to move on. Something in me yearned for more depth to my life, and after talking to my pastor I announced to my parents that I was going to transfer to the Lutheran college just outside of Chicago. There were closer Lutheran colleges, but I knew too many students there. Deep within me, I felt a need to start out where nobody knew me so I could discover who I really was. Although concerned about my being so far from home and about the finances, my parents supported my decision. I am eternally grateful for their trust in God in this matter. (Actually, I did have one friend at River Forest, but since she already had a roommate, I felt I was pretty much on my own.)

WHAT IS FAITH?

Once in the new school, it didn't take me long to change my major from English to theology with the goal of becoming a director of Christian education with an emphasis on youth work. During my three years there I took a closer look at who I was and what I wanted out of life. I began to question the organized church (in a safe sort of way). Sunday morning services at the church next to the campus held no appeal for me. (Was that because it appeared large and impersonal when I was used to a small congregation or that I just needed to be rebellious? I don't know.) I enjoyed attending the Wednesday night folk mass on campus and a small inner-city worship setting. This was a small rebellion compared to what many experienced in the early '70s, but for me, I was charting new ground. I thoroughly enjoyed my theology classes. For the most part, the professors encouraged the students to think. They refused to accept the pat "Sunday school answers" and challenged us to dig deeper to find personal meaning to some of life's oldest questions. The Bible was the foundation for study, but the building supplies were works of numerous Christian theologians, some of whom did not take a Lutheran point of view.

During this time I also experimented with behavior that was not God pleasing. Once again, compared to some people my age during that time, my excursions might seem fairly safe, but my mother would not have approved, and I knew I was on dangerous ground. In spite of what I did, I never felt that God had abandoned me or even that I had abandoned God. I knew He didn't approve of much of my behavior, but I believed He loved me regardless of my sin. I didn't feel that it was all right to sin because God forgives. I just strongly felt that He would be there to pick me up when I fell. I knew there would be consequences to pay, but forfeiting His love was not one of them.

God blessed me in spite of myself, for He sent a good man my way. We fell in love and got married the summer before our senior year. Tim had also been raised in the Lutheran church and had a background similar to mine. Yet our faiths seemed very different. My God had personally intervened in my life many times, and I felt very close to Him. To me, Tim's relationship with God was not so much personal as private, and I didn't quite understand that. As a child he had attended a Lutheran school but not gone to Sunday school, for which I mockingly ridiculed him. (He wasn't to blame. His church was so large that the congregation organized Sunday school for those children who did not attend the day school.) He preferred a large church; I like a small intimate one. His family left for home minutes after the benediction was spoken; mine was often one of the last to leave. I had been actively involved in youth activities; he had occasionally attended youth functions. We believed in the same God, but our way of living our faith seemed very different.

When we graduated, Tim received a teaching assignment but I didn't. Somehow this didn't seem quite right to me. He wanted to be a Lutheran school teacher, but deep down, I wondered how much his low draft number influenced that desire. I thought I would be a great youth director/DCE with all of my high school experiences, but I found that not many churches wanted to hire a female DCE in 1973. I knew my future was in God's hands. I couldn't quite believe that if only one of us were to get an assignment, it would be Tim. On top of that, he was called to teach just outside of New York City. I wanted to return to southern California. I cried for three weeks.

In mid-July I was still in disbelief at this turn of events. I still hadn't received a call to be a youth director, and we were packing up to move to New York and wondering where I would work. I missed my family, I missed my friends, and I felt that God had missed the boat by not providing me with a wonderful job. Toward the end of the month we received an unexpected phone call. A teacher at Tim's school had left without warning; would he like to move to seventh and eighth grades, and would I teach fifth and sixth grades? Instead of being grateful for a job, I talked the principal into letting me teach the seventh and eighth graders. (When he wasn't sure at first, he asked me to tell him about myself. The only thing that came to mind was, "I'm short." God worked through that response, because he hired me.)

Even though I had never planned to teach, I found I loved my seventh and eighth graders. Being in New York, the last place I wanted to be, became a major blessing in my life. Tim and I became members of that small congregation and learned to share our faith with each other. Since our staff was small and we knew few others outside of our church and school, we grew closer. Our pastor and principal and their wives became trusted friends with whom we could talk politics or theology and even disagree. When our son was born and we moved west, I realized that I had grown in many ways through our New York experience.

WHAT IS FAITH?

Tim served as principal of a small urban school and four years later received a call to start a school at a relatively new congregation. This church was made up of many young families who immediately reached out to us. A woman's Bible study group insisted I join them, and our study and fellowship bonded us into a tightly knit group. My feelings of belonging to a group had not been that strong since I had participated in high school youth activities. I experienced God's love through their care and concern.

After six years of "retirement" from teaching while my two children were small, I decided it was time to return to the classroom. During those six years, I had done substitute teaching in many of the area's Lutheran schools, and many of those schools had inquired if I would be interested in a full-time job. Since Tim and I had worked well together at our school in New York, I wanted to work with him again. However, one school board member was opposed to having spouses on the same staff. I prayed about this situation and believed that God would soon influence the member to change his mind. God saw fit to answer my prayer with "Wait."

The next few months were difficult. I was mad at my husband because he wasn't able to change the board member's mind. I was mad at the church because I thought they should hire me anyway. But mostly, I was mad at God. It was going to be hard enough to adjust from being a full-time mom to teaching full-time with all the mom duties on top of it, but now I had to go through this hassle. At about the same time I was dealing with my father whom I loved but who had decided he no longer wanted to live with my mother. What was God trying to do to me here?

Finally, after weeks of ranting and raving at God and whoever else would listen, I gave up. I turned to my Bible and poured over it looking for verses that seemed to apply to my situation. Every time I found a meaningful selection, I wrote it on an index card until I had a stack of cards about half an inch thick. Whenever thinking about the situation overwhelmed me, I would get out my stack of cards and just start reading through them. God calmed me through His Word until I eventually could think about the situation without being reduced to tears. Finally the board member changed his mind, and I got the job.

For the next nine years, I often thought I knew what members of the early church felt like. This congregation was strong in worship, God's Word, fellowship, and service. Our school staff was extremely cohesive. A small group of families, ours included, started camping together and strong friendships developed. Our group wasn't perfect in our faith walk, but we had great fellowship and worshiped together while out in God's wilderness. One husband, who was a fairly new believer, once shared with us, "You're the only group of people who ever just accepted me as I am and didn't try to change me." Over the years we camped together, we saw him grow spiritually. I think the group's acceptance was an important aspect of his growth.

Then Tim received another call to a school with a long history and great potential. As much as I didn't want him to leave our congregation, I knew God was calling him to be in this new place. He commuted to the new school 17 miles away, and I stayed in my classroom. At that same time, several other personnel changes occurred at my school. Some of the members of our camping group moved out of the area. Within a year, it seemed like a totally new place, one where many of the teachers no longer felt comfortable.

Later our community of believers broke up, probably due to many factors. Our school and church staff was torn apart with a strong rift between teachers and administrators. I struggled to find God in the situation. He seemed strangely silent. I was angry at the individuals that I blamed for the problem. Their profession of faith seemed much different than their actions. A battle for control turned into a spiritual crisis for me. To make matters worse, my pastor was my adversary. I decided the situation would never be resolved and ran to my husband's new school. Did I abandon my trust that God has the ability to reconcile? I was afraid to confront that question for fear of what I would answer.

For the next few years, I felt that my faith was on "automatic pilot." It was a dry period. One of the last things my former pastor said to me was, "No matter what happened, I knew it would never affect your faith." But he was wrong; it had. My heart felt weak like it was no longer capable of strenuous Christian love for others. I questioned why God had allowed the problem to escalate to such large proportions. I had seen my colleagues beaten down and broken. It was a situation where no one won. In the end almost every staff member involved left the congregation, which also had major healing to do.

Through all this one thing stood out. My husband became my spiritual guide. His faith has grown in dramatic ways since we were married 24 years ago. When I couldn't talk to God, he listened and spoke God's healing words to me without placing blame for the problem. When I couldn't pray, he prayed for me and with me. He stood by me when I felt I was in a spiritual abyss and constantly reassured me that God was with me in my hurt. The "head" knowledge that had been taught to me at a young age never left, but the heart is still recovering.

The past few years have been a rebound period for me. For the first two years after I escaped the problem, I felt numb. My "head" knew God hadn't left me, but my heart didn't feel His presence. The experience was painful but perhaps necessary for future growth. This time has been a transition time. Just like our time-keeping, I think I had to fall back before I could spring ahead. My heart is beginning to experience God's love again, and I'm excited about sharing my faith with others. I'm still at my husband's school, although he has left to work at the university level. I feel God is leading me in new directions, and I eagerly anticipate discovering where He wills me to be.

A REFLECTION

Writing my story of faith was an enlightening experience for me. At times in my life my head knowledge seemed to secure me to Christ. That knowledge was a firm foundation on which I could stand, even when my heart knowledge was frail and weak. On the other hand, when the heart seemed to be in control my faith appeared to soar. Those are the spiritual highs in my life for which I am thankful.

What do *I* think faith is? Faith is an assurance that God is there for me. As the writer to Hebrews says, *Now faith is the assurance of things hoped for, the conviction of things not seen* (11:1 RSV). This assurance did not originate within me; the Holy Spirit placed the seed of faith in my heart at my Baptism. This faith does not make sense to those who don't have faith. In fact, it's hard to understand it logically because it is beyond human understanding. But I know it's real. In addition, I have been blessed with certain conditions that promoted the growth of that seed. Along with God's Word, my Baptism, and the Lord's Supper, the Holy Spirit used my Christian upbringing with strong "head" emphasis and the support of Christian relationships to sustain my faith.

The times when I have felt especially close to God revolve around strong Christian relationships. The communion of saints, the community of believers that have spoken God's Word to me, has upheld me on many occasions. This has not been limited to the "up" times of life. My closest friend's mother died the day after my father's funeral. It was a time for sorrow, but never did I feel despair. Surrounded by caring Christians in my congregation, my husband's congregation, my father's congregation, and Carol's congregation, I experienced an extremely strong assurance that God was working in both Carol's and my life with His unconditional love.

In Bible study God draws me closer to Himself and strengthens my faith. However, I have to admit that I have low tolerance for a surface study where participants lack the trust to be honest with each other. Personal prayer and Bible study time on a regular basis have always been important to me, but I struggle with time commitments to make time for God. (It goes back to my sin-stained priorities and how I choose to spend my time.)

Meaningful worship is another faith fuel. The liturgy, whether traditional or contemporary, strongly speaks Law and Gospel and reflects my dependence on Jesus. Since a liturgical tradition was part of my upbringing, nonliturgical worship seems empty to me or at best like "worship lite."

Opportunities to live my faith in service seem to serve as faith fertilizers. For me this service seems to require an unselfish commitment of my time, and being both a busy and selfish person, I find this personally challenging. I can rationalize just about anything to avoid forfeiting something I really (selfishly) want to do.

The biggest challenges to my faith have occurred when I have separated myself from other Christians and from God's Word. Wrapped up in my problems, I have failed to seek Christians who were little Christs to me. Doing so has cut me off from those who knew when I needed to hear Law and when I needed to hear Gospel. Even though I'm a visual person, hearing God's Word spoken to me personally has been more meaningful than just reading my Bible.

Now, after all this self-examination, I return to my earlier question. Did I first have trust that led to a desire for knowledge or did trust follow knowledge? Although trust came first in my life, I'm not sure it works that way for everyone. I believe God placed me in a home where it was easy to learn trust. My parents provided for me. My siblings loved me. My needs were met. From infancy I trusted that the world would be a safe place based on my earliest experiences. My parents made sure I had knowledge early in life. I spoke simple prayers before I had true understanding. I heard Bible stories. Spiritual traditions were part of my life even before I was able to participate or comprehend them. Later, in my teen years, I experienced trust on a much deeper level. On the other hand, God's love was taught to me at a very early age. That knowledge has grown through the years. If ever I were to decide that I "know it all" when it comes to God, I'm sure my faith will stagnate.

So what do you think? Where does faith start? Can you retrace the path on which your faith has carried you? Where did your faith start and in what manner has it grown? Take some time to examine your faith life. Then share it with someone else and watch that faith grow.

My Personal Faith Journey

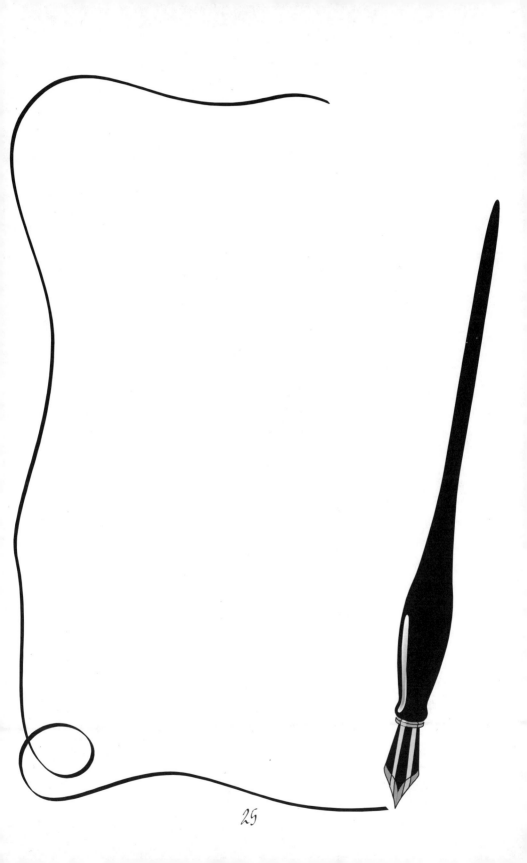

What Is Faith? God Speaks

Now that you've read all that, you've heard enough about me. It's time to move to another side of the block, the most important side. This side of the block reveals what God says about faith in His Word. We will examine what God tells us about faith, ponder how it is obtained, explore how it grows, investigate its benefits and rewards, and evaluate the input the individual has in his or her faith.

The Bible is filled with numerous references to faith and stories of faith. However, only one verse clearly defines faith. That verse begins Hebrews 11, often called the faith chapter of the Bible: *Now faith is being sure of what we hope for and certain of what we do not see.* The writer of Hebrews continues this chapter with a list of believers who lived in the certainty of God fulfilling His promises even when all human evidence worked contrary to it. As well as listing men and woman of faith, these verses reveal a number of characteristics of faith.

Before you continue reading these words, grab your Bible and a pencil. Read for yourself what God says about faith in Hebrews 11. As you read jot down what these verses tell you about faith. Don't worry about coming up with eloquent statements; just rephrase what we discover about faith from the brief stories the writer tells.

FAITH DEFINED AND DESCRIBED

Hebrews 11:1 defines faith as a confidence that is deeply rooted in one's innermost being. This confidence is not easily explained to those who lack faith, for the experience of faith is not evident to unbelievers even though it is obvious to believers. The Revised Standard Version uses the words *assurance* and *conviction* to describe faith: *Now faith is the assurance of things hoped for, the conviction of things not seen.* These two words emphasize the strength of faith for the believer.

If I am assured of something, it is like having a guarantee. The object of my assurance is all but in hand. It is secured now, but not quite yet. There is no reason for me to doubt. Usually strong assurance is based on someone's past performance of which I have either first- or secondhand knowledge.

In the case of the believer's assurance of eternal life, God has fulfilled many promises along the way. Even though I have not yet experienced heaven, I have experienced His unconditional love in my life and seen its effects in the lives of others. I know how over-powering His peace is. This love and peace is often felt most pro-foundly in the midst of a major crisis. He has reassured me that He truly does work for the good of those who love Him. He has pro-tected me and loved ones in dangerous situations when reason dic-tated that injury should have resulted.

Let's examine the word *conviction.* When a person is convicted in a courtroom, the judge or jury is convinced that he or she is guilty of a crime. A convict has been proven guilty. The word *convict* comes from the word *convince.* Convince means to overcome the doubts of another or to persuade by argument or evidence. If you dig a little deeper, the word is derived from the Latin word mean-ing "to conquer." God the Holy Spirit works faith in our hearts as He conquers our doubts and fears. These doubts and fears are replaced by the conviction that He who created this universe out of nothing (Hebrews 11:3) can conquer any danger out there, just as He has already conquered sin, death, and the power of the devil through Jesus' death on the cross.

The reading of Hebrews 11 reveals several truths about faith as illustrated in the lives of believers. We will review these truths and also investigate some other Bible references that explain what faith is all about.

FAITH PLEASES GOD

Verses 2–6 of Hebrews 11 declare that faith pleases God. When Abel presented an offering to God in faith, God was satisfied and pleased. Cain had also offered a sacrifice, but his gift was given for all the wrong reasons. There was no love supporting his donation, no motivation of thanking God for His many blessings, no gratitude for God's goodness. Cain was going through the motions and doing what was expected only because it was expected. Abel, on the other hand, gave the best of his flock because God had provided His best for him. Abel gave a thank offering; Cain gave only a display, but he did not fool God.

Without faith, our actions do not impress God no matter how sacrificial they may appear to others. Faith is the doorway by which we gain access to God. Verse 6 reminds us, *Without faith it is impossible to please God, because anyone who comes to Him must believe that He exists and that He rewards those who earnestly seek Him.*

THE OBEDIENCE OF FAITH

Another aspect of faith becomes readily apparent in verse 7. Faith obeys God. When Noah looked around at his environment, he saw a barren, landlocked region. No pleasure or fishing boats dotted the landscape. Sea gulls did not soar over his surroundings. Yet he built the ark trusting that God would provide the water it would need to do what boats do. He obeyed even when it meant suffering the ridicule of friends and neighbors. God told Noah to build a ship larger than a football field, coated with pitch inside and out, and topped with a roof. Then he was to fill it with two of every creature and the food needed to feed them. No small job. Genesis 6 reports that Noah obeyed. We have no clue of what the weather was like when God issued His holy command. But Noah obeyed. God's Spirit was at work in him enabling him to complete the job God placed before him.

In Romans 1:5 Paul wrote of calling the Gentiles *to the obedience that comes from faith.* Faith allows the believer to obey even when obedience looks foolish in the eyes of the world. Abraham also obeyed God's command as explained in verses 8–10 of Hebrews 11. In some ways, the obedience of Abraham is even more amazing than that of Noah. Noah was a God-fearing man who walked with the Lord. But Abraham probably did not know God. His father probably worshiped the moon-god, as Joshua 24:2 explains. Abraham likely worshiped as his father did. But then God told him to go to the land He would show him. Abraham would be leaving his relatives and all that he knew. He was asked to follow the directive of a God he did not know, whose faithfulness was unproven in his own experience. And then, Abraham obeyed. God had promised to make a great nation of Abraham's descendants. Abraham believed and looked to the time the promise would be fulfilled. That's confidence!

FAITH BELIEVES PROMISES

Hebrews 11:11–16 points out how faith holds to promises. Faith trusts that promises will be kept and not forgotten or broken. Those promises might appear to be as preposterous as the belief that a 100-year-old man and a 90-year-old woman would have a baby. Sarah was barren; she had given up on having children years before. Abraham is described "as good as dead." The chances of this couple having a child seem utterly ridiculous. But this same man had trusted God's word to travel far from his home to a new country, where his descendants would be as numerous as the stars in the desert sky. Abraham was not a young man when this promise was given, yet he left all that he knew to see the promise fulfilled. Abraham did not live to see just how thoroughly God accomplished this end, but he did live to see his son Isaac marry Rebekah, knowing that God was at work in the lives of his descendants.

FAITH IS TESTED

Hebrews 11:17–19 teaches us that faith is tested. Once again the writer uses the example of Abraham. Abraham's son, Isaac, must have been the light of his life. Looking at his offspring must have always brought a smile to his face for his son was the embodiment of God's love for him. What could have gone through Abraham's mind when God announced that he was to sacrifice his long-awaited son as a burnt offering?

Genesis does not record the patriarch's thoughts, but it does report his actions: the next morning Abraham saddled his donkey, cut wood for the fire, and set out for the destination God would reveal. He took his son and two servants with him. When he told the servants to wait while he and Isaac went up to the mountain to worship, he said, *We will come back to you* (Genesis 22:5). When Isaac asked him what they would sacrifice, Abraham confidently responded, *The Lord will provide*. Yet Abraham never faltered in doing what God had commanded. They reached their destination. They built an altar. The wood was piled on it. Abraham tied up Isaac. He placed his much loved son on the altar. He raised the knife to slay his son. The test revealed Abraham's total reliance on God, and God provided a ram to sacrifice in place of Isaac. In faith Abraham faced reality; yet he looked beyond it to see God and His promises. Faith is tested. Expect it.

FAITH IS FULFILLED IN THE FUTURE

Hebrews 11:20–22 communicates that faith realizes that not every promise is fulfilled today, not every prayer is promptly answered with a yes. Faith looks to the future for fulfillment. The mass of Abraham's descendants were born after his death. When Joseph died in Egypt after living most of his life there, he left instructions for his bones to some day be carried to his homeland. The Egyptians had him embalmed and placed in a coffin in Egypt. However, centuries later, Moses carried out this request. The Old Testament believers waited for the Messiah but never saw Him. They looked to the future for this prophecy to be fulfilled, and they gave glory to God that He would do as He had promised. They were blessed for trusting that it would certainly happen.

FAITH ENDURES SUFFERING

Verses 23–28 reveal that faith endures suffering. Moses had the opportunity to live a life of luxury and prestige. He chose to leave that life and be identified as a Hebrew, one who was marked for death and who should have died if the Pharaoh's orders had been carried out. His people were confined to slavery. Their lives consisted of servitude and suffering. Forced to flee from Egypt to save himself from the Pharaoh's wrath, Moses returned when God commanded it. Even though Moses doubted his own abilities, he took God at His word that He would assist him. He left his new life in Midian for one that would include 40 years of wandering in the wilderness and much discontent from the people he led. His faith enabled him to live a rather miserable and frustrating 40 years.

Countless other Old and New Testament believers suffered for their faith. The writer of Hebrews implies (in verses 32–38) that the list is too long to individualize, but when the faithful suffered for their faith, they were blessed. Indeed, he states, "the world was not worthy of them" (verse 38). Faithful believers endure suffering.

FAITH EXPECTS THE UNEXPECTED

Faith sees the unexpected as disclosed in verse 30. Miracles happen. Joshua led the Hebrews into the Promised Land only to find it occupied. By following God's battle plan (which must have seemed completely absurd to anyone trained in military tactics), the city was taken without the loss of Jewish blood. God said, "March around the city once every day for six days, and on the seventh day march around it seven times. Blow the trumpets and shout." When they did so, the walls of Jericho fell down. The city was theirs.

Believers saw the mouths of hungry lions shut, the faithful protected from flames licking their toes, and the dead raised. Faith expects the unexpected, because God doesn't have to follow the rules imposed on the natural world. Faith believes that God is beyond human and natural limitations.

JESUS FULFILLS FAITH

Finally, verses 39–40 allude to the fact that faith is fulfilled in Jesus. Jesus shows the love of God the Father to us. If we want better to understand what God is all about, we need only to look to Jesus. Jesus personifies God because He *is* God. If you know Jesus, you know God. Our faith is rooted in the fact that Jesus is one with the Father. Jesus fulfilled all the requirements for salvation and bestows the benefits of salvation on all those who believe in Him. The Holy Spirit inspired the books of the Bible to be written so that the story of God's love can be shared. The apostle John summarized this by writing, *But these are written that you may believe that Jesus is the Christ, the Son of God, and that by believing you may have life in His name* (John 20:31).

As stated earlier, *Faith is the assurance of things hoped for, the conviction of things not seen* (Hebrews 11:1 RSV). It is the act of believing the unprovable deep in one's heart. It is the God-given ability to trust that He will provide for all one's needs. It is knowing by the Spirit's instruction that God is the author of creation and the means of salvation through Jesus Christ. Faith is more than a noun, more than just head knowledge that Jesus is Lord, more than just some "baggage" Christians carry with them. Faith is a way of life that spills into every aspect of life.

If Hebrews 11 were the only word from God about faith and what it means in the life of a believer, we would know quite a bit about this phenomenon. But God doesn't limit our base of knowledge about faith to 40 verses. Throughout the Bible inspired writers reveal pieces of faith to us. Let's look at some of these.

LIVING IN FAITH

Saul was determined to see the Christians destroyed. But then this man with a mission experienced such a profound event that he even changed his name to indicate the extent of the transformation he personally underwent. He was no longer the same person; he experienced a total rebirth. Saul became Paul, the apostle of Jesus Christ. He referred to the pervasiveness of the Christian faith more than once. In Galatians 2:20, he said, *I no longer live, but Christ lives in me. The life I live in the body, I live by faith in the Son of God, who loved me and gave Himself for me.* Paul could no longer separate himself from his faith in Jesus. On the road to Damascus his life changed, and it would never be the same again. Faith became his new way of life. He could no longer look around without his faith impacting what he saw. God in Christ had taken him over, and he was a new person.

This experience extends beyond St. Paul. In Romans 1:17, Paul declared, *The righteous will live by faith.* Living in faith becomes the way of life for all believers. Through Baptism God gives all Christians new life. More than something Christians "do," this is a blessing bestowed when the Holy Spirit works faith in our hearts.

Fowler's picture of faith as the lens through which we view our world makes sense. When I look around without my corrective lens, everything is a blur. Things are not really what they seem, and I miss much that is actually there. But once my contact lenses are in, the blurs sharpen into recognizable objects. When I view the world through eyes of faith, everything comes into focus. I see the world as it truly is, and I become aware of all that God does for me. I see the need for God's love in the lives of unbelievers, and I aim at sharing His love so that they, too, can see Him clearly.

The thought of sharing one's faith with others makes some Christians nervous. They worry if they will say the right thing. They wonder if the time is right. They fret over the results of such sharing or lack of them. But that uneasiness over sharing one's faith is unfounded. There's no reason to place this burden of anxiety on your own shoulders. Even the apostle Paul admitted, *I came to you in weakness and fear, and with much trembling. My message and my preaching were not with wise and persuasive words, but with a demonstration of the Spirit's power, so that your faith might not rest on men's wisdom, but on God's power* (1 Corinthians 2:3–5). God uses us in our weakness; our frailties speak to His strength. The most articulate and expressive speaker can do nothing to further God's kingdom unless the Spirit is working in the hearts of the listeners. We find this demonstrated in Ephesians 2:8–9: *It is by grace you have been saved, through faith—and this not from yourselves, it is the gift of God—not by works, so that no one can boast.*

COMING TO FAITH

Christians need to share the message of God's salvation with others. Romans 10:17 states that *faith comes from hearing the message,* and every Christian has the privilege of helping broadcast God's message. But then our responsibility ends. God the Holy Spirit takes over. The Spirit works faith in the hearts of unbelievers. God does this purely by grace, not because of any deserving qualities within the individual. One can do nothing to earn a gift; a gift is simply that, a gift, given by the generosity of the giver.

Ephesians 2:9 shows that the faith sharer is not the faith worker. The faith sharer is simply the medium through which the message is delivered. The gift is God's message of salvation through Jesus Christ. At most the faith sharer might be considered to be the giftwrap. In no way does the giftwrap indicate the quality of the gift. Therefore, the faith sharer acknowledges that faith is God's gift, not something he or she has accomplished in the heart of the unbeliever. The faith sharer cannot boast of his or her "conquests" for Christ. Only by the work of the Holy Spirit can another individual come to faith.

The Holy Spirit works through the Word and the sacraments to bring faith to unbelievers. For some people faith begins when they hear the Word of God being preached. This preaching can take place in a formal worship service or in the quiet witness of a Christian neighbor who daily lives according to faith until the unbeliever asks, "What is it that makes the difference in your life?"

The accounts of the gospels reveal that many came to faith just by observing Jesus and what He did. After Lazarus was raised from the dead, many put their faith in Jesus. The book of Acts is filled with many accounts of people wanting to be baptized after hearing the disciples preach and seeing their boldness for Christ. This tells us that knowledge is important. Without it, faith would falter. Perhaps knowledge could be considered to be a fertilizer of faith. The Ethiopian asked Philip to explain the Scriptures to him for "how could he understand it unless someone explained it to him?" Once he understood that the prophet Isaiah was talking about Jesus, he asked to be baptized.

However, if faith were only a matter of gaining knowledge, we would have little need for the Holy Spirit's input. God makes it very clear in the Scriptures that the Holy Spirit works faith in human hearts. The Jewish Christians in Galatia insisted that the Gentile Christians had to follow certain Old Testament requirements. Paul responded to this falsehood in Galatians 2:15–16, *We who are Jews by birth and not "Gentile sinners" know that a man is not justified by observing the law, but by faith in Jesus Christ. So we, too, have put our faith in Christ Jesus that we may be justified by faith in Christ and not by observing the law, because by observing the law no one will be justified.* Paul continued in Galatians 3:3 by clearly pointing out the influence of the Holy Spirit in the origin of faith: *After beginning with the Spirit, are you now trying to attain your goal by human efforts?* Paul makes it clear that faith begins with the Spirit's work; it is not a human accomplishment.

In 2 Thessalonians 2:13 Paul again reiterated that people are saved through faith, which is activated and maintained in a person's life by the Holy Spirit. *But we ought always to thank God for you, brothers loved by the Lord, because from the beginning God chose you to be saved through the sanctifying work of the Spirit and through belief in the truth.* The work of the Holy Spirit is to bring people to faith and then empower them daily to put their faith into action in obedience to God's will revealed in His Word. Paul counsels Christians how to live so that the light of salvation shines through us. 2 Corinthians 3:3 reminds us, *You show that you are a letter from Christ ... written not with ink but with the Spirit of the living God, not on tablets of stone but on tablets of human hearts.*

THE FAITH OF BABIES

While faith for some people might begin with hearing God's message, for others it begins in infancy when there appears to be little or no comprehension of the spoken word. A newborn cries from discomfort. Gentle hands help and hold. The infant responds to his mother's face because trust has been established in a relatively short time. Although the baby cannot grasp the meaning of the knowledge of God, through the work of the Holy Spirit faith in God is instituted in Baptism. In Psalm 22:9–10, David wrote, *Yet You brought me out of the womb; You made me trust in You even at my mother's breast. From birth I was cast upon You; from my mother's womb You have been my God.*

Obviously we humans cannot understand exactly how this is accomplished. Yet we can confidently say that the baptized newborn is clearly a part of God's kingdom of believers. Granted faith through the working of the Holy Spirit, the infant has been justified and lives as one of God's chosen, even without apparent head knowledge of God. Faith in God has been planted in the child's heart. *For it is with your heart that you believe and are justified* (Romans 10:10).

Of course, parents, godparents, and the congregation have the responsibility to see that the message of God's love is shared even before the child can fully comprehend it. Mark records that people brought their children to Jesus so He could bless them. Knowing Jesus was tired, the disciples discouraged the parents from approaching Him. When Jesus saw what was going on, He was indignant. He said, *Let the little children come to Me, and do not hinder them, for the kingdom of God belongs to such as these* (Mark 10:14). Then He blessed them. There's no documentation that these children understood all that was happening. But Jesus understood how important it was to build on the faith that the Spirit had begun.

Timothy came to faith at an early age. Through the influence of his mother and grandmother, his faith continued to grow. In 2 Timothy 1:5, Paul writes to Timothy, *I have been reminded of your sincere faith, which first lived in your grandmother Lois and in your mother Eunice and, I am persuaded, now lives in you.* Through the daily living of their Christian faith, mother and grandmother impacted the heart knowledge that was being developed in Timothy.

Christian parents and role models exhibit their faith not only by what they say, but also by what they do in the ordinary and extraordinary events of their lives. Timothy's faith resulted from the Spirit's work in his life and in the lives of his mother and grandmother. They did not just leave the growth of his faith to chance, hoping he would "catch" it; they taught him from a young age what God had done for him. 2 Timothy 3:14–15 details the influence of this early instruction: *But as for you, continue in what you have learned and have become convinced of, because you know those from whom you learned it, and how from infancy you have known the holy Scriptures, which are able to make you wise for salvation through faith in Christ Jesus.* Although Jewish boys received formal instruction beginning at age five, Lois and Eunice did not wait until this time to begin sharing their faith with Timothy. And what a blessing this proved to be in Timothy's life!

THE GROWTH OF FAITH

Scripture explicitly states that faith does not remain static, but grows and develops. Paul shared his hope to extend his borders of influence beyond the Corinthians as their *faith continues to grow* (2 Corinthians 10:15). He complimented the Thessalonians on the evidence he'd heard of their faith maturing. *We ought always to thank God for you, brothers, and rightly so, because your faith is growing more and more, and the love every one of you has for each other is increasing* (2 Thessalonians 1:3).

As a seedling grows into a tree, changes take place. The seedling is delicate and fragile. Its thin stalk can break; it can be easily bent to grow in a distorted shape. Its survival is better assured if it is protected and nurtured. As it grows it becomes stronger. Its branches fill out and provide shade. It becomes sturdy and can weather the elements. In due time it brings forth fruit.

The faith of a new Christian, whether a small child or a newly converted adult, is much like that young seedling. An immature faith can be easily bent or broken by the forces around it. It needs to be protected and nurtured by immersion into God's Word and an environment of faithful believers. Paul confessed, *Night and day we pray most earnestly that we may see you again and supply what is lacking in your faith* (1 Thessalonians 3:10). As faith develops, Christians share their faith. This, in turn, leads to more growth. Paul the evangelist had a clear appreciation of this concept, *I pray that you may be active in sharing your faith, so that you will have a full understanding of every good thing we have in Christ* (Philemon 6). Mature faith can hold up to the storms of life and does not waver when the future looks bleak. In Romans 5:3–4 Paul explained, *We also rejoice in our sufferings, because we know that suffering produces perseverance; perseverance, character; and character, hope.* As faith grows, one can see evidence of its development through the Christian love shown to others. Knowing the power of the positive, Paul commended the Colossians for their faith. *We have heard of your faith in Christ Jesus and of the love you have for all the saints* (Colossians 1:4).

Faith grows by the power of the Holy Spirit working through study of the Word and the encouragement and influence of other believers as they share God's Word in worship and fellowship. God declared the importance of knowing His words in Deuteronomy 11:18–21: *Fix these words of Mine in your hearts and minds; tie them as symbols on your hands and bind them on your foreheads. Teach them to your children, talking about them when you sit at home and when you walk along the road, when you lie down and when you get up. Write them on the doorframes of your houses and on your gates, so that your days and the days of your children may be many.* The Hebrews took God's command literally and did exactly as He instructed. In following the meaning of this edict, we can never take for granted that we know everything about the Bible and the message it brings. We can never assume that children will learn about God when they are ready. We can never feel that personal Bible study is not important in the life of the Christian. We can rejoice that God made His Word clear to us through the Bible. We can thank God for corporate Bible study and the blessings it brings. We can be assured that time spent in Bible study is never wasted.

Perhaps one of the greatest blessings God gives to us here on earth is the communion of saints, the fellowship of believers. The Christians that surround us in our congregations, workplaces, and neighborhoods are there for a reason. Paul often commented on how Christians build up each other in the faith. He acknowledged that other believers uplifted him in his faith walk. He knew that he had an impact on the faith of others through the power of the Spirit. He often spoke of his desire to meet with specific Christians. *I long to see you so that I may impart to you some spiritual gift to make you strong—that is, that you and I may be mutually encouraged by each other's faith* (Romans 1:11–12).

Faith grows through imitating the lives of the faithful. Nowhere does the Bible tell us to revere these faithful human beings as people free from sin; however, Paul knew that Christian leaders could do much teaching by their example. This method can have a positive domino effect as it did in Thessalonica. *You became imitators of us and of the Lord; in spite of severe suffering, you welcomed the message with the joy given by the Holy Spirit. And so you became a model to all the believers in Macedonia and Achaia. The Lord's message rang out from you not only in Macedonia and Achaia—your faith in God has become known everywhere* (1 Thessalonians 1:6–8). The writer of Hebrews stated, *Remember your leaders, who spoke the word of God to you. Consider the outcome of their way of life and imitate their faith* (Hebrews 13:7).

When Christians become complacent in their faith, the danger of falling away from God becomes apparent. Hebrews 6:1–12 warns believers of not desiring spiritual maturity. Some people are content never to learn more about God other than the basics. They fail to see the importance of exercising their beliefs by putting their faith into action. This failure for faith to thrive can lead to spiritual death. Paul wrote, *Therefore let us leave the elementary teachings about Christ and go on to maturity. ... We do not want you to become lazy, but to imitate those who through faith and patience inherit what has been promised* (Hebrews 6:1, 12). Through the prophet Isaiah, God reminded His people of the need to hold steadfast to their faith. *If you do not stand firm in your faith, you will not stand at all* (Isaiah 7:9).

THE RESULTS OF FAITH

Can we identify faithful believers? Only One can absolutely determine who has faith in his or her heart, and that is God Himself. We know that *the Lord does not look at the things man looks at. Man looks at the outward appearance, but the Lord looks at the heart*

(1 Samuel 16:7). God reminds us that He *searches every heart and understands every motive behind the thoughts* (1 Chronicles 28:9). As Christians who trust in an omniscient God, we can be thankful He does not ask us to judge whether or not one has faith.

Although we do not evaluate whether another has faith, God admonishes each of us to look at our own heart and appraise the faith found there. This exercise can lead to spiritual growth at any point in one's life. Paul wrote, *Examine yourselves to see whether you are in the faith; test yourselves* (2 Corinthians 13:5).

When we review our own faith, we do not simply measure our head knowledge and scriptural facts. This does not discount the blessings and benefits that result from Bible study. Indeed, the more time we spend in the Word, the more the Spirit works to increase our understanding. However, the writer of the book of James (probably James the brother of Jesus) preached strong words about the measure of faith. *What good is it, my brothers, if a man claims to have faith but has no deeds? ... Faith by itself, if it is not accompanied by action, is dead* (James 2:14, 17). Martin Luther explained this by saying that a person is justified by faith alone, but not by faith that is alone. When one has true faith in God through Jesus Christ, Christlike actions will result. God does not require us to follow specific rituals. As pointed out earlier, we do not earn salvation by what we do. But, as Paul pointed out to the Galatians, *The only thing that counts is faith expressing itself through love* (Galatians 5:6). Genuine faith shows in what one does for others; it is active in doing for others. God might be the only One who sees some of the acts of love; yet each individual Christian knows the content of his or her heart and how that is expressed.

Sometimes the Christian's faith does falter. Sometimes we find we have drifted away from God and that our lives have spun off course. When this happens, God calls us to repent and turn aside from our destructive course and receive Jesus' invitation, "Come to Me." Ignoring the warning signs—a lack of concern for others or actions that reveal no love—can have disastrous results. Paul reported to Timothy that some had rejected God *and so have shipwrecked their faith* (1 Timothy 1:19). However, when we see these warning signs, we can have hope that God has not abandoned us. Jesus knew that the disciples would have their faith tested. Even the confident Peter, who was sure he would never forsake Jesus, was not immune. When Jesus warned Peter of the impending events surrounding His crucifixion, He added, *But I have prayed for you, Simon, that your faith may not fail. And when you have turned back, strengthen your brothers* (Luke 22:32). God uses even our weaknesses of faith to benefit others.

THE BLESSINGS OF FAITH

First and foremost, where faith is found, salvation is found. God promises release from the judgment of the Law and clothes Christians with the righteousness of Jesus. God no longer looks at the sinner, but instead He sees the perfection of Jesus draped over the believer. A heavenly home with God for eternity awaits every Christian who faithfully confesses that Jesus is Lord. There can be no greater blessing.

But the promise of a blessed eternity is not the only blessing God grants to Christians. *By faith we ... receive the promise of the Spirit* (Galatians 3:14). The Holy Spirit empowers believers to do great things for the Lord. Jesus promised, *I tell you the truth, if you have faith as small as a mustard seed, you can say to this mountain, "Move from here to there" and it will move. Nothing will be impossible for you* (Matthew 17:20). This verse does not promise that Christians will necessarily perform miraculous feats and gain great fame. Rather, it means that faith will enable one to do things the particular individual would have never been able to do without faith. The shy introvert will freely share Jesus with others. The brash, gruff leader will quietly and gently comfort a friend. The possibilities are endless.

Faith protects against the wiles of the devil. Even though Christ has won the victory against Satan, the evil one will not rest until he has done all the damage he can do in this world. He measures victory in souls that refuse the gift of saving faith. If he can turn a believing heart into a rejecting heart, he receives even greater joy. But faith arms Christians for the battle against the devil. Paul knew the dangers of the devil's power and advised the Ephesians to *take up the shield of faith, with which you can extinguish all the flaming arrows of the evil one* (Ephesians 6:16). Once again, faith enables us to rely on a power that is not our own.

Faith keeps our priorities in line with God's priorities. In following God's will for our lives, we have a peace that only those who have experienced it can understand. Paul explained this by writing, *Since we have been justified through faith, we have peace with God through our Lord Jesus Christ, through whom we have gained access by faith into this grace in which we now stand* (Romans 5:1–2). We often describe God's peace as the peace that passes understanding. Christians have often described times of immense turmoil in their lives as those times that they have felt this peace most strongly. Nonbelievers are often drawn to the peace that believers radiate.

SOME CONCLUDING THOUGHTS

Faith is powerful! In this chapter we have looked at just a few of the many scriptural references to faith. We know that faith enables the believer to please God through obedience and love. Faith will be tested in this world, but God promises that He will never allow Christians to suffer more than they can bear. In faith we enjoy the blessings God gives us now, look forward to future blessings, and also acknowledge that God works in unusual ways that we don't always anticipate.

Talk to 20 different people about their journeys of faith, and you will hear 20 different stories. While our experiences of faith have similarities, each story is unique. The Holy Spirit works in each person's heart and life in a distinctive way. Some people come to faith in infancy, others during childhood or the teen years, and others as adults. No matter when one comes to faith, we all desire greater spiritual maturity.

Faith enables people to do mighty works for God's glory. Faith produces the armor that helps fight off temptation. Although the Spirit is the faith-worker, God gives every individual Christian the responsibility to live in that faith. Faith becomes especially vulnerable when we take it for granted. A strong faith is active. Such faith brings blessing not only to the individual Christian but also to those within the Christian's circle. Christians are indeed blessed to be a blessing. Praise God!

ON YOUR OWN

This chapter's research on faith does not claim to be all-inclusive. You can discover much more about faith through personal Bible study. Using a concordance, read and ponder other references about faith. Try words such as *heart* and *belief.* What other truths about faith do you find?

Try writing a journal entry applying one of the thoughts in this chapter to your life. In other words, write about a time your faith was tested, or how God answered a prayer in an unexpected way, etc. Share your story with someone else.

Some Thoughts about Faith

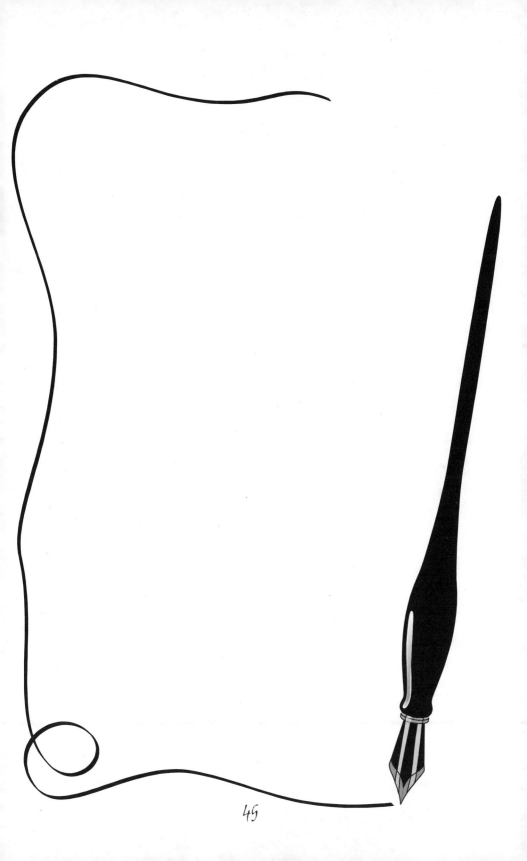

Cognitive, Psychosocial, and Moral Development

It's time to turn the block of faith to reveal a new side. This face contains the names of three researchers: Jean Piaget, Erik Erikson, and Lawrence Kohlberg. These men all investigated how children develop into mature adults. Piaget focused on cognitive development, that is, how children's thinking and intellectual processes change. Erikson studied psychosocial or personality development. Kohlberg examined moral reasoning, or how children determine right and wrong.

You may ask, why read about secular development theory when the topic is faith and how it grows? The answer is simple. Faith is not a compartmentalized part of life that can be biopsied as a separate component of a person. True faith is integrated throughout the whole person. It cannot be separated from the intellect, the personality, or one's sense of morality. The work of Piaget, Erikson, Kohlberg, and others have strongly influenced the work of James Fowler, whose life work revolves around faith development and whose theories we will explore in chapter 4.

The work of these researchers also can benefit anyone working with children. Piaget's work details what children can and cannot do and understand. Teachers of preschoolers through young adults benefit from applying cognitive theory to their lesson plans. From Erikson we learn what types of feelings and behaviors are considered normal for each age. His work gives cues on appropriate teacher responses to students of various age levels. Kohlberg's research gives teachers insight into how children define right and wrong. Behavior adults consider obviously to be moral behavior may be judged as unacceptable to a young child, and what a young child considers to be logically correct might sound outrageous to an adult.

PIAGET AND COGNITIVE DEVELOPMENT

Jean Piaget was a Swiss psychologist who lived from 1896 to 1980. He believed that children's thinking processes develop in stages. These stages are typically found at certain ages, although the ages aren't exact and frequently there are deviations. The stages are sequential; one cannot enter stage three thinking without going through stages one and two. He maintained that these stages are universal without regard to sex, class, or culture.

Piaget concluded that the mind operates differently at different ages. The way a 5-year-old understands concepts differs from the way a 14-year-old makes sense of his world. Yet every human has a basic need to organize new information; this is how we learn and mature in our thought processes.

When new information doesn't seem to fit into our organized way of thinking, we use either assimilation or accommodation to make it fit. In using assimilation a young child might call a whale a "big fish," because things that live in the water are called fish. Even though she might be told that a whale is a mammal, not a fish, this new information will probably not immediately change her way of thinking of the whale as a big fish. Only over time as she also encounters seals, sea otters, and other sea creatures will she be able to acknowledge that some animals that live in the ocean are not fish. This process is called accommodation. The child has developed a new category of animals that live in the ocean other than fish.

Piaget developed four stages of thinking. The ages assigned to each stage can vary for different individuals; yet every individual goes through the stages in the same order. Sometimes people will use a more advanced way of thinking, and sometimes they revert to a simpler form. Moving from one stage to the next is not a leap into sudden understanding but a gradual process. The characteristics of each stage are explained below.

Sensorimotor Stage

This stage occurs from birth to about two years old. Young children learn about their world primarily through sensory impressions and physical activities. A young infant recognizes that objects within his sight exist. Once an object drops out of view, it no longer exists in his way of thinking. Usually by about eight months of age, he recognizes that when he can't see an object it is still somewhere, and he will search for it. Around six to eight months the infant will scream for his mother when he realizes she isn't around. We see this ability as an important milestone in thinking skills. As the child grows, he begins to use more and more mental functions. Imitation of people and animals is commonplace. Being able to bark without having a barking dog present is an achievement in learning. The child is learning to use symbols or words in his thinking.

Preoperational Stage

Most two- to five-year-olds fall into this stage. "Operational" refers to logical thinking. The Preoperational Stage occurs before children are capable of using logic. This stage builds on the characteristics of the previous stage. Children in this stage of cognitive development work on the mastery of symbols, most often words, which allows them to gain from past experiences.

We find a good example of this thinking in what is probably Piaget's most famous experiment. If you show a preschool child two identical containers holding an equal amount of water, the child will agree that the amount of water is the same. However, if the water from one container is poured into a narrower, taller container, the child will say that the taller container holds more water. The child is not able mentally to reverse the action of pouring the water back into the original container. She can comprehend only one feature of the water at a time. Children of this age would argue that the taller container must have a greater amount of water. Older children, who are capable of reverse thinking, would understand that although the water level is higher in the taller, narrower container, they both hold the same amount.

Sometimes preschoolers seem self-centered when asked to consider the feelings of others. However, the average four-year-old cannot take another person's point of view. Her thinking processes reveal that she thinks everyone else thinks the same way she does.

Concrete Operational Stage

Seven- to 11-year-olds move into the Concrete Operational stage of thinking. Children now understand that matter can take different shapes and forms. They can form related classes of items. They are capable of arranging objects in a particular order. However, this works only with items the child has experienced in the past or if the child has the concrete object in front of her as she works with it.

The majority of seven- and eight-year-olds would understand how the water in a tall, narrow glass could be the same amount as held in a shorter, wider glass. But they would usually have trouble applying the same idea to a piece of clay that could be molded into different shapes without experimenting with the clay themselves. Normally by the time children are 11–13 years old, they will successfully solve abstract problems of this type.

Formal Operational Stage

At around age 11, children begin to use formal operational thinking; however, not until about the end of high school do most become proficient at it. In this type of thinking, children do not need to manipulate concrete objects to come to conclusions.

In one of Piaget's experiments with adolescents, he provided a basin filled with water, a set of metal rods of various lengths, and different weights. The basin was made so that various rods could be attached to the side of it. The goal was to use the weights to bend the rods just enough to touch the surface of the water in the basin. Using trial and error the adolescent will discover that with differing weights the rods longer than four inches will all touch the water, but no combination of weights will result in the four-inch rod touching the water. Formal thinkers will deduce that if the four-inch rod will not bend, neither will the two- or three-inch rods. Concrete thinkers will have to do the actual experiments to discover this. A proficient formal operational thinker will be able to form hypotheses, do mental calculations, and test the most logical theories all in his/her mind.

Sometimes adolescents get "bogged down" considering all the possible solutions to a problem. (Compare this to the preoperational thinker who can only understand the situation in front of him.) At times all the possible abstract ideas will obscure the obviously realistic conclusion. With maturity, adolescents learn to sort idealistic solutions from the more practical, reasonable ones.

Also at this age we find a new form of the preschooler's inability to take another's point of view. Adolescents often view life through the opposite extreme. They imagine everyone sees themselves the same way they do. Hence, if they feel "stupid," everyone must think they are stupid. If they think they are having a "bad hair day," everyone probably thinks they look awful. No wonder youth feel so self-conscious during the teen years.

Not everyone agrees with Piaget. Some researchers feel that he focused too much on what children cannot do rather than on what they are capable of doing. Some theorize that young children have more advanced thinking abilities than Piaget believed, and that adolescents do not learn formal operational thinking as early as he thought. While most experts agree that the order of the stages of cognitive development is universal, some conclude that different cultures have different rates of development. Some specialists question whether the formal operational stage is found in all cultural groups. In spite of the controversies and questions, most still consider Piaget one of the world's foremost authorities on how people learn.

What implications does Piaget's work have for both professional and volunteer teachers in religious settings? We will address specific suggestions for each age group in our concluding chapters. For now, think about a few basics.

Children do seem to move from one stage to the next in a predictable sequence. Do not ask children to do something that is beyond their range of reasoning. Direct your classroom activities to what the students at that age level are able to do. However, never forget that individuals mature in their abilities at different rates; you will have a wide variety of ability levels within one class. Therefore it is wise to offer an assortment of activities to appeal to all of your students.

ERIKSON AND PERSONALITY DEVELOPMENT

Erik Erikson began his life's work with Sigmund Freud. However, a variety of experiences in different parts of the world influenced him in ways that moved him beyond Freud's theories. Erikson concluded that social and cultural factors determine much in the development of one's personality. These factors include the values, attitudes, beliefs, and customs of one's society.

A human fetus develops in an organized predictable manner to be a normal baby by the end of a nine-month pregnancy. Erikson believed the personality underwent growth in similar stages to become a mature adult. Just as Piaget's cognitive stages were sequential, Erikson's psychosocial or personality stages occur in the same order in all individuals; although, again, he assigned general ages to his stages with expected deviations. He identified eight stages of psychosocial development. In order to move from one stage to the next, the individual must resolve a crisis between positive and negative forces. Let's take a look at Erikson's stages of personality development.

Trust vs. Mistrust

In a baby's first year of life, either she learns to trust or she doesn't (mistrust). When parents or other caregivers consistently provide for her basic needs of hunger, comfort, and care, she learns to trust her world. She feels secure in the knowledge that she is loved and will be cared for. This feeling will permeate all the other relationships in her life.

However, a baby will also experience instances when no one immediately provided for her immediate needs. Most people have seen how a young child will cry for her mother and mother only. Until Mommy appears, there is no appeasement. These type of experiences lead to mistrust. Note that experiencing some mistrust is necessary for healthy personality development. If a child learned only trust and never considered that there are some situations and people one ought not to trust, life would indeed be a dangerous journey.

Erikson believed that religion helped to build a person's sense of trust. When we know God is present and working in our life, trust is strengthened. Recognition of evil in the world supports feelings of mistrust. The knowledge of a strong loving God enables one to overcome the negatives in one's life.

Autonomy vs. Shame and Doubt

The two- to three-year-old child wants to do everything for himself. The transition from stage 1 to stage 2 is marked by the growing sense of independence and the battle of *no!* Even parents with the best intentions of allowing their children age-appropriate independence must at times say no to the wants and efforts of the child. Anyone who has spent any time with two-year-olds knows that the most frequently used word in their vocabulary is no (possibly because they have heard it so frequently?).

Parents must allow their child to try things for himself while providing proper supervision. Parents who are impatient with the child's efforts and do too many things for the child that he needs to learn to do himself can hinder the child's growth. Not being allowed to try things for himself, he begins to doubt that he is capable. Parents who are overly strict often end up raising a child plagued by shame. He believes that even when he tries something on his own, it won't turn out right and he's ashamed of his attempts.

The conflict of Autonomy vs. Shame and Doubt in a child's life sets the stage for the role of obedience to God throughout life. Willing obedience to God can happen only in a positive relationship where one knows forgiveness is available for the times we fail to follow His will. Overly demanding parents can steer a child into believing there is no way to please God even through faith.

Initiative vs. Guilt

The four- to five-year-old child not only has more mastery over her vocabulary and actions, she also has an active imagination as well. One of the tasks of this age is to discover what kind of person she can become. Her imagination can allow her to be anything she wants to be—mother, father, doctor, fire fighter. Because the imagination is so fertile, she sometimes has difficulty separating fantasy from reality.

A child enters this stage when she has successfully integrated her desire to do things for herself with her parents' need to give adequate supervision. She is now ready to take the initiative. A sense of responsibility and accomplishment guide her actions. When she meets her goals, her sense of self-worth grows. She sees the world as a friendly place.

Of course, not every attempt at initiative ends successfully. The process of learning to do things for oneself often proceeds through a process of trial and error. When failure occurs, guilt often follows. Sometimes parents, teachers, or other caregivers ignore or criticize success. When this happens, the child feels guilty that she even tried to use her initiative. If the guilt becomes too overwhelming, it will defeat her ambition, and she will cease trying new things.

Loving parents who know God forgives failures through faith in Christ Jesus, and continues to love in spite of fiascos, have a powerful influence on their children's motivation to try new things. They forgive when messes are made. They allow the child to clean up after himself. They listen to and answer their children's questions. They avoid restricting their children or making them feel foolish for trying things on their own.

Industry vs. Inferiority

The 6- to 11-year-old is characterized by imagination and curiosity. Children of this age want to discover things for themselves. They need to be encouraged to make articles and learn information on their own. Even if attempts are unsuccessful, they need to be praised for trying and guided to the knowledge that mistakes can be valuable learning tools. Elementary-aged children identify heroes and imitate those they admire. When they succeed, they develop a sense of industry. They believe they are capable people, and their self-confidence grows.

On the other hand, inferiority results when he is not allowed to pursue tasks on his own or his attempts are belittled by adults or older children. He does not value intellectual growth in himself or others. He might grow to believe that he cannot do anything well on his own and sometimes even stops trying. Parents of a child this age need to allow him to do things at his level and not try to improve them to an adult level. Parents should supervise school projects but not do them. The process becomes more important than the product.

Religious education of children this age can present a challenge. They want and need to do things on their own. Teachers ought to provide opportunities for them to make and do. However, the teacher must continually teach that our worth in God's eyes is not connected to our successes in life. We cannot earn God's love through our efforts. Through Christ He loves people in spite of their mistakes, failures, and downright disobedience. Spiritually we all have to admit, "We can't do it ourselves," and thank God that He has done it for us.

Identity vs. Role Confusion

Twelve- to 18-year-olds search for their identity. During this time they strive for independence from parents and grow physically. The search for identity of the individual has been developing since infancy, but suddenly the quest becomes central to her life. She seeks to match the identity given by her parents and family up to this point with the identity as seen by others, most notably peers. This confirmation by self and others can be either positive or negative. We may see her either as a productive member of society or as a delinquent.

Figuring out who she is leads to self-assurance and confident decision making. She knows who she is and where she is headed. This sense of well-being makes commitment possible. Even though she may feel conflicting loyalties, she will be able to be faithful to her self-determined direction.

When she has trouble finding her identity, role confusion results. This is especially true in sexual and vocational identity. Hence, she will have no clear idea of acceptable behavior that would be confirmed by others. This has been further complicated by the changing role of women in our society. Without going into an involved discourse on this topic, suffice it to say that parental guidance is crucial for both males and females to reach their God-given potential.

This stage can be considered critical in faith development, for one prays that the adolescent confirms her identity as child of God and makes a personal commitment to her Lord. This might relate to a formal public ritual of confirmation in the church or a more personal and private declaration of faith. A person cannot skip this stage and continue to grow in spiritual maturity.

Intimacy vs. Isolation

The young adult seeks intimacy with another person. Intimacy means the deepest commitment that can be shared between two people (although not necessarily sexual) or between a person and a cause or concept. From intimacy comes love. In this context love is the ability to give of oneself without the fear of losing the self; it differs from infatuation or lust. Erikson argued that people cannot experience love until this stage of development.

The individual cannot achieve intimacy until he has firmly established his own identity. If he fails to find intimacy, isolation results. Isolation causes one to reject others and their ideas and even "destroy" them if they appear too threatening. Thus the individual closes himself off from others.

This stage has many ramifications for one's faith life. Christian community and fellowship are based on achieving intimacy within the household of faith. To fully understand what the communion of saints is all about, a person must achieve intimacy with other Christians. To experience all the blessings of a Christian marriage, one must overcome isolation and learn to be intimate with one's spouse.

Generativity vs. Stagnation

Erikson defined generativity as the need to have and raise a family. It can also refer to a person's life work, what she hopes to leave to the next generation (teaching, doing biological research to further environmental causes, etc.). This stage covers the longest period of one's life, generally from the early 30s to the middle 60s.

Care becomes evident during this stage. Parents care for their children and guide them to growth as productive members of society. People in the work force care for the product they create or the service they provide. Problems arise when a person takes no pride in her occupation or volunteer activities. If she sees no purpose or benefit to what she is doing, she views her work as drudgery. When people fail to care, they stagnate.

The adult who faces stagnation becomes self-absorbed. This becomes more and more likely in our highly complex society. A high divorce rate, separation of extended families, and the expectation of putting long hours into the job all cut family connections that encourage care. Modern technology often separates the worker from the finished product and does not provide that experience of taking pride in the job. Work overload causes the service worker to feel overburdened and stressed. When we feel we don't make a difference, we become passive.

The message this stage brings to religious education is powerful.

Churches must provide opportunities for members to put their faith into caring action. Christians need to feel they are making a difference in their world; that is our mission. As we reach out to others, we serve God. When we show no caring concern for others, faith stagnates. Stagnating faith is in its death throes.

Integrity vs. Despair

In the senior years, the individual faces the fact that one's life will soon be over. This knowledge results in either integrity or despair. If the individual can look back on his life and feel he has contributed something worthwhile, the feeling of integrity emerges. Wisdom is found in those who have found psychosocial integrity. However, despair will reign if he sees little of value achieved. It is now too late to try something new. Fear of death is evident; for many, that marks the final failure.

A Christian finds integrity in the trust that heaven is just around the corner. The faithful individual has a hope that is not just wishful thinking, but a solid commitment to the home Jesus has prepared. He can look back on a life in which God has made a difference. He praises his Lord for the times he has been used to make a difference in someone else's life. However, for the non-Christian, the idea of death offers nothing but despair, for hope is nonexistent.

Not all researchers agree with Erikson and the methods he used to generate his theory of personality development. Most researchers demand the use of test methods that give precise results. Erikson based many of his ideas on personal observation. Some human behavior experts feel that his stages of development are more accurate for males than for females. Carol Gilligan reworked the stages for girls and found that different issues affect different ages. Other experts believe that the childhood stages are too similar, with each revolving around children's abilities to do things. However, a familiarity with Erikson's theories will benefit teachers in a number of ways.

At this time, we would just remind the reader that it is important to remember that different types of behaviors are common at different ages. The responses teachers make to student behaviors can influence children either positively or negatively. Specific suggestions for particular ages will come in later chapters.

KOHLBERG AND MORAL DEVELOPMENT

Lawrence Kohlberg was just out of high school when he was faced with moral decisions that involved helping Jewish refugees after World War II. After being frustrated in what he felt was his inability to make good judgments, he enrolled in college and pursued a doctoral degree in clinical psychology. From his research he identified six stages of moral reasoning, or the way people decide between right and wrong. Kohlberg was influenced by Piaget, but he went beyond the work Piaget had started on moral development. Since his original work, Kohlberg has revised some of his theories, yet he still feels his stages of moral development are sequential and universal. One cannot skip stages. Not all individuals reach every stage, but all people go through the stages in the same order.

Kohlberg identified three levels of moral reasoning: Preconventional Morality, Conventional Morality, and Postconventional Morality. Each level contains two stages.

Kohlberg believed Preconventional Morality, which refers to the inability to understand the rules of a society, is found in children up until about the age of nine. Conventional Morality is found in 9- to 20-year-olds. They obey the rules of society precisely because they are the rules. The last level, Postconventional Morality, is found only in adults, but Kohlberg felt that not all adults reach this level of reasoning. He would explain that some adults never progress beyond stage 2 or 3. People of any age might be found in the "lower" stages. The name *Postconventional Morality* refers to understanding the moral ideas that support society's rules.

Level 1: Preconventional Morality
Stage 1: Punishment-Obedience Orientation

For this person the wrongness of an action is determined by the physical punishment incurred. Motive is not a factor in determining if something is right or wrong. Accidentally knocking over an entire display of cans in the grocery store is worse than getting mad and breaking a vase intentionally. Authority figures should be obeyed because if you don't, you will get in trouble. Obedience is right because that is the way you avoid punishment.

Stage 2: Instrumental Relativist Orientation

An action is thought to be right if it brings about results that benefit the person doing the action. This often involves an even exchange. "If I do what the teacher wants, she will treat me fairly." Justice is viewed as fairness. Rules and laws are important to the person in this stage. Obedience directly benefits the individual. This sometimes leads one to believe that right behavior should always be rewarded.

Level 2: Conventional Morality

Stage 3: Mutual Interpersonal Expectations, Relationships, and Interpersonal Conformity Orientation

An action is judged to be right if it pleases or impresses the people who are important in one's life. Authority (which depending on one's viewpoint can be found in a variety of places) and conformity are respected. Obedience pleases other people.

Stage 4: Social System and Conscience Orientation

At this stage a person views an action to be right if it obeys the rules of the authorities and helps to keep order in the social system. Obedience is seen as one's duty. Rules are established by the authorities and must be respected.

Level 3: Postconventional Morality

Stage 5: Social Contract Orientation

An action is judged to be right if it brings about "the greatest good for the greatest number of people." Authority is not obeyed just because it is the authority but because people have mutually agreed that the laws will benefit most people. The rights of the individual are important and not to be discarded. At this stage of reasoning, civil disobedience is acceptable if it is necessary to help others.

Stage 6: Universal Ethical Principle Orientation

In this stage of moral reasoning, which Kohlberg himself admitted was an ideal that rarely if ever is actually found in real life, one must decide by which moral principles one will live. (Principles differ from rules and laws in that principles are the overriding guidelines by which rules and laws are made. The Golden Rule is considered a principle.) These principles would be considered just and fair to all involved, no matter what their background. The stage 6 person would consistently live by these principles even if he does not directly benefit from them.

There are many critics of Kohlberg's work. Some researchers say that his findings are descriptive of American males but do not always apply to other cultures or to American females. Kohlberg believes that moral development can be hastened through teaching. Not all other experts agree 'with this. Some say the dilemmas he presented for classroom discussion are so far removed from students' lives that the application has no practical use.

In teaching for moral development, other specialists suggest using realistic stories or newspaper articles that present the moral decisions people have to make in life. (Should there be government restrictions on the amount and type of violence shown in video games? What rules should cover keeping alive aged people who have no hope of living without the assistance of machines?)

Finally, we need to be asked whether moral thinking affects moral behavior. Children's moral decisions tend to change when the circumstances change. Research has shown that moral instruction that focuses on memorization without a child understanding the meaning of the instruction is basically worthless.

How does this apply to religious education? The most obvious message is that memory work alone will not change a child's sinful nature. Teachers need to realize that primary-aged children will react differently to moral struggles than high school students. Educators can present realistic moral dilemmas for student discussion. Students need to be allowed the freedom to offer their ideas without the immediate correction of the "right, Christian" answer. They should be encouraged to explain why they think as they do. After discussing one situation, the teacher can change it slightly and have the class discuss whether changing the circumstances would change the decision made. Finally, the Christian educator can assist her students in recognizing that God's Word is the Christian's highest moral authority. Sometimes, the best question to ask might be, "What would Jesus do?"

CONSIDERATIONS

This chapter has presented much information that has been researched by educational and psychological experts; however, we must remember that research is continually occurring. Sometimes two "experts" examining the same question will appear to generate two opposing conclusions. Research guides teachers; it doesn't mandate particular teacher behaviors. It can be a starting point for your own personal research based on the students in your classroom.

What to do with all this scholarly information? Get together with a group of your colleagues and discuss the findings of Piaget, Erikson, and Kohlberg. From your own experiences, which theories seem to hold true and which do you have trouble accepting? How do these theories agree or conflict with what we find in God's Word? What specific applications most relate to the students you teach?

In our next chapter we will see how Piaget, Erikson, and Kohlberg have influenced religious education researchers, and how these researchers agree and disagree among themselves.

Stages of Human Development

Approximate Ages	Piaget	Erikson	Kohlberg
Infancy (0-2)	Sensorimotor	Trust vs. Mistrust	*Preconventional Morality (0—9)*
Early Childhood (2—6)	Preoperational	Autonomy vs. Shame and Doubt Initiative vs. Guilt	1. Punishment-Obedience Orientation
Childhood (7—11)	Concrete Operational	Industry vs. Inferiority	2. Instrumental Relativist Orientation
			Conventional Morality (9—20)
Adolescence (12—21)	Formal Operational	Identity vs. Role Confusion	3. Mutual Interpersonal Expectations, Relationships, and Inter-personal Conformity Orientation
Young Adulthood (21-35)		Intimacy vs. Isolation	4. Social System and Con-science Orientation
			Postconventional Morality (20—)
Adulthood (35—60)		Generativity vs. Stagnation	5. Social Contract Orientation
Maturity (60—)		Integrity vs. Despair	6. Universal Ethical Principle Orientation

Faith Development Theories

We now examine the fourth side of the block of faith. Let's see. The first side we looked at contained the author's story of faith. By now we hope the reader has also journaled and shared his or her own story of faith. Next, we investigated what the Bible says about faith. In the previous chapter we studied the theories of three human development experts. Now we will explore what religious education researchers propose in their theories.

Of course, we will never know every angle of faith. To do so would presume that we human beings have full understanding of the mystery of faith. It would signify that we completely comprehend God's wisdom. But that claim cannot be made. As 1 Corinthians 2:4–5 explains, *My message and my preaching were not with wise and persuasive words, but with a demonstration of the Spirit's power, so that your faith might not rest on men's wisdom, but on God's power.* Mere mortals cannot begin to perceive God's power. God demanded of Job, *Who then is able to stand against Me?* (Job 41:10) while clearly pointing out that He is more powerful than any of His creations. Recall the words of 1 Corinthians 13:12: *Now we see but a poor reflection as in a mirror; then we shall see face to face. Now I know in part; then I shall know fully, even as I am fully known.*

"Help!" you might be saying. "I want to discover what faith is all about. I want to know how best to teach in order to help my students' faith grow." Rest confident in God's wisdom. He gives us what we need to know. Remember, the Holy Spirit gives faith and guides that faith. He will use us in spite of our weaknesses and our lack of understanding.

That being said, let's examine the fourth side of the block. And although this book focuses on children and their faith, we will cover all of the proposed stages of faith, even those that relate to adults.

FOWLER'S STAGES OF FAITH

James W. Fowler earned his Ph.D. from Harvard University. Many people consider him to be one of the world's foremost experts in the psychology of religion and the study of faith development. Fowler would identify himself as a Christian (coming from an Episcopalian background), a minister, a teacher, and a counselor in addition to being a researcher. Although not all other Christian researchers agree with his theories, most would admit to the influence of his work. He, in turn, has been influenced by the research of Kohlberg, Erikson, and Piaget among others. Like them, he believes that people move through stages in life that are sequential and universal. Through countless interviews with a variety of subjects, both Christian and non-Christian, some claiming to be religious and some identifying themselves as atheists, he identified six stages of faith.

Fowler would say that these stages of faith are universal. He believes that they fit any religion whether it is Christianity, Islam, or Hindu. He contends that even those who profess to be atheist or agnostic would conform to a stage of faith, because everyone puts his or her trust in something. He explains faith as the way one gives meaning to the dynamics of life; therefore, everyone gives meaning to life in some manner, even those who profess to be non-religious.

Every stage of faith builds on the previous stages. People always go through the stages in the same order. One cannot skip a stage; however, it is not unusual for people to regress to a previous stage. Sometimes they will move back more than one stage. Some will remain in the "lower" stage for the rest of their lives; some will continue to advance through stages after a brief respite at a lower stage. Not all people progress through every stage. According to Fowler, members of some denominations tend to remain at a certain stage. In his views, Lutherans often move to stage 3 and stop their development there.

Moving from one stage to the next does not depend on one's age. People of any age can be found in stages 1 or 2 faith. Chronological age, intellectual development, and psychological maturation will all influence the stages of faith but not determine them. Transitions are usually marked by some sort of crisis that might actually jeopardize one's faith. Hence moving to a new stage is often painful and usually confusing as the individual begins to make meaning of his life in a new way. Sometimes it might even seem that he has lost his faith. (More on this later.)

Each stage of faith is characterized by specific patterns of thinking. (The content of faith is not an issue here.) It is important to remember that no stage of faith is "good," "bad," or better than another. Since stages reflect different thinking methods, the level is not a judgment of one's faithfulness. In no way should we consider a level 4 stage of faith superior to a level 2 stage, or a stage 1 purer than stage 3.

Why should religious education teachers study Fowler's stages of faith? Probably most of our teaching has to do with the content of what we believe more than how we think about our faith. We teach about Jesus, how God impacted the lives of Bible characters, and how He interacts with people today. We want our students to know the Lord and to trust Him. We desire that they grow to a deeper faith life. Yet if teachers understand how children and adults think about their faith, we can more easily provide experiences through which they grow in spiritual maturity. Let's investigate Fowler's stages of faith.

Infancy and Undifferentiated Faith

Fowler does not identify this period in an infant's life as one of the stages of faith. However, it is at this point that he believes one's pre-images of God begin. He calls them pre-images because they are formed before the child begins to use language or think in concepts.

Fowler builds on the position of Erikson, who identified this age as Trust vs. Mistrust. The infant's world revolves around having basic needs met. As food and comfort are provided, the mother or other caregiver bonds with the baby. The child begins to trust that the parent will provide what is needed in life, while at the same time she experiences love, hope, and courage. This forms the basis for the trust experience she will later develop with God. On the other hand, if these needs are not met, or provided with great inconsistency, the opposite is learned. Food might be provided, or then again not. The infant begins to develop the idea or feeling that no one can be trusted. Also if the child's needs are constantly provided before she even realizes the want, she might believe that the world revolves around her. This outlook on life would pervert her view of the world as well. At about two years of age, when she begins to use language and think about her play, she moves into stage 1.

Stage 1: Intuitive-Projective Faith

We typically find this stage of faith in two- to six- or seven-year-olds, although people of any age can possess stage 1 faith. A young child's image of God will likely be connected to his image of his parents. Mommy and Daddy, or his primary caregivers, are the most powerful people in his life. If they have been warm, loving, and forgiving, the child will probably see God that way. If they have been overly busy and neglectful, the child will view God as noninvolved with the world. If the parents have been strict and harsh in dealing with the child, he will be afraid of God. If the child witnesses his parents making God a priority in their lives, spending time in prayer, and participating in regular worship, the child will take these values for his own during these years.

If you recall Piaget's Preoperational Stage, you'll know that young children cannot yet use logic. Their thinking is not reversible, and they cannot view things from another's viewpoint. Four-, five-, and six-year-olds have an active imagination. For them, fantasy is often the same as reality. They often string together pieces of unrelated stories and have misconceptions about the stories and facts they are told.

Fowler believes that it is important to provide a rich background of Bible stories that are nonthreatening to a young child's way of thinking. For instance, Fowler would suggest that parents and teachers of children ages two to seven avoid stories that emphasize God's wrath. We would say, however, that you should not feel that stories with "bad" events will damage the child. Hearing the story of the flood can reinforce the belief that God takes care of His children. Teachers, parents, and others need to allow children the opportunity to retell freely these stories or act them out to help clear up any misconceptions or threatening information.

Reflect back to the story of Jesus and the children. Jesus knew His time connecting with them was well spent. What was important here was not that they understood in a cognitive way that Jesus was God, but that they were touched and blessed by a loving authority figure, a Very Important Person. Jesus had time for them. Jesus cared about them. Jesus blessed them. In time they would make the connection that God has time for them, God cares about them, and God will bless them.

Stage 2: Mythic-Literal Faith

At about age seven the individual begins to be capable of concrete operational thought and usually moves into the next stage of faith. Although this stage is most typical of the elementary-aged child, we also see adolescents and adults at this stage.

Children of this period consider fairness to be extremely important. Probably the biggest complaint of eight- and nine-year-olds is, "That's not fair!" The best treatment from others (whether peers, teachers, parents, or God) is what is thought to be fair in the child's eyes. The concept of fairness is his way of making sense of the world. Kohlberg identified moral behavior of the school-age child as that which brings about an even exchange. The saying "You scratch my back; I'll scratch yours" can even lend itself to a child's image of God. To the child's way of thinking, if he obeys God, God will cause good things to happen to him. When bad things happen in his life, he blames himself and tries to identify where he went wrong.

At this age the child also loves to tell long, detailed stories. He is capable of filtering the real from make-believe. The ability to retell another's story accurately or to fabricate a story that flows and makes sense helps him to order his life (although it often tries the patience of an adult listener). However, as much as the storytelling ability has developed since the preschool years, the child still cannot "step outside" of the story to give meaning to the symbols found in it. Stories tend to have literal interpretations. When asked to describe God, the child will do so in human terms: flowing robe, long white beard, etc.

One of the pitfalls of this stage of faith is that the child is inclined to be very moralistic. "If you are bad, you will get punished. If you don't get punished, you must be good." This way of thinking can lead to a works-righteousness attitude, where the children incorrectly believe they can earn their own salvation. Children in this stage often have a hard time recognizing and admitting their own sinfulness.

A stage 2 person relates better to stories of Law than stories of Gospel. They see God as a judge who takes care of wickedness. This reinforces one's idea of fairness. The concept of a forgiving God who doesn't always give people what they deserve (no punishment to suffer; forgiveness is offered) is not always "heard" or understood by children at this age. They more readily accept the story of the thief on the cross, who had to die for his sin but was taken to heaven (punishment suffered and forgiveness offered).

The disciples who asked Jesus why the man had been born blind displayed stage 2 thinking. They were trying to make sense of why bad things happen to people. To their way of thinking, the man or his parents must have sinned. They could not comprehend another reason for this terrible fate. If something bad (blindness) had occurred, it must be the result of a sin committed. The "average" person with stage 2 faith is often an elementary-age child. To their way of thinking, bad behavior generates punishment and bad things happen; good behavior results in rewards and blessings. Children at this age are concrete in their thinking. Object lessons appeal to them.

Stage 3: Synthetic-Conventional Faith

We often find this stage of faith in the 12- to 18-year-old; however, according to Fowler, many remain in this stage for the rest of their lives. Several factors assist the transition from stage 2 to stage 3. As adolescents begin to develop formal operational thinking, they acquire the ability to step outside of the stories they tell and give meaning to them. They can reflect not only on the past, but also can compose pictures of the future. They now understand the perspectives of others to the extent that the significant others in their lives (frequently, their peers) will become so important that many, even most, decisions are made on the basis of what these others think.

The typical teenager is a conformist. She is looking for a group with whom to identify. This might be friends, organizations, or parents. For those who have been raised in the church, the doctrines they have been taught since infancy can become clearly identified as one's own. However, they may not have carefully examined those doctrines and values. Rather, they may have accepted the belief system because it has been accepted by others who are important in their lives.

Youth at this age have a need for friends who know them intimately, accept them, and affirm the person they are becoming. The need for acceptance and affirmation applies to God also. They view God as a friend, counselor, and guide. They rejoice in God, who knows all about them and loves them anyway. With the development of formal operational thinking, they can begin to conceive of an omnipotent, omniscient, and omnipresent God. These characteristics of God can be extremely reassuring because adolescents are aware of their own limitations and inadequacies. Their relationship with God who knows but loves and accepts anyway can be a crucial factor in the process of developing their own identity.

Fowler calls stage 3 faith a tacit system; that is, an unexamined way of thinking. A person with stage 3 faith will be able to describe and detail her beliefs; she will earnestly defend her faith when challenged; she has a strong emotional involvement with her religion. But she will not be able to explain why she believes as she does, because she has not reflected on her faith. She accepts her beliefs because significant others in her life (parents, friends, the organized church) accept and promote their beliefs.

Stage 3 Christians respond to Bible stories that emphasize God's love and forgiveness. Since stages 1 and 2 thinking forms the basis for stage 3 thinking, these youth can relate well to stories that have both Law and Gospel. They are able to rejoice in the fact that God isn't fair and that we don't get what we deserve. The idea of the Christian community is especially appealing to them as relationships are vital in their lives.

Reflect back to the story of Saul. He personified stage 3 faith in his identification with the Jewish leaders. He was taught by one of the most respected authority figures of his day and took Gamaliel's belief and values system as his own. Saul's close sense of belonging with the leaders who wanted to safeguard their beliefs against the Christians motivated him to make it his personal mission to destroy this errant group. He considered Jewish history and wanted his church to remain as it had been for centuries. The Christians were a threat. His faith required that he eliminate that threat; he had no interest in discovering for himself who Jesus really was.

According to Fowler, many members of mainstream churches stay in this stage throughout their adult lives. The church often does not encourage questioning of its accepted practices and values. Acceptance of the church's doctrinal stance is expected, even required. To question is to "rock the boat" of one's faith. Some even think it is dangerous to question—what if one "falls out of faith"?

The transition to stage 4 faith commences when the individual begins to reflect on and critically examine her belief system. Often this is related to "leaving home" either physically by attending college or emotionally when one breaks some of the emotional bonds with one's parents. Other factors that lead to a transition are a conflict between authority figures or a marked change in policy by church leaders or other religious authorities. (The changes in the Catholic Church after Vatican II prompted many within that church body to examine critically their faith.) Saul began the transition to stage 4 faith when he encountered a clash between authority figures: the Jewish leaders versus Jesus, whose authority was substantiated by the fact that this crucified man appeared as a light from heaven, spoke to him, and blinded him. Thus Saul was primed for a new way of thinking.

Stage 4: Individuative-Reflective Faith

The transition to stage 4 faith often takes from 4 to 10 years. This stage comes at a time when many leave home in one way or another. It might occur when a young adult goes off to college. It might happen when one joins the army or independently moves out to get a job. For some it happens later in life, with the death of a parent, a divorce, or a major job change. Suddenly, the individual is looking at life in a new way.

A person entering stage 4 begins to examine values and beliefs that he has accepted for years. He is often physically separated from the groups that have given him his identity up until now. At this point in life he begins to investigate who he really is and what he believes. Instead of relying on external authority, he perceives an internal authority. He still sees the group with which he chooses to identify as important, but their values and beliefs are subject to what Fowler calls the "executive ego." Now the self becomes the authority that scrutinizes the opinions and actions of others. One begins to learn to accept his own judgment without relying on others.

The individual at this stage of faith examines the symbols that have been important to him and questions their meanings. When this happens, he no longer views the symbols themselves as sacred. He often feels a sense of loss. Trying to sort out his thinking, he might experience grief and even guilt. To some, even himself at times, it appears as if he has lost his faith. If this transition comes in later adulthood, the stress and struggles associated with it are even more keenly felt.

A stage 4 person does not necessarily reject the content of his faith; he just begins to think about it in a new way. He no longer accepts his church doctrines because the church authorities, his parents, or friends in the church expect him to. He has struggled with examining why he believes as he does and often desires to keep these beliefs because they make sense in his life. Rituals and symbols might not have all the mystery they once held for him, but they have become meaningful in a new way. The person evaluates Bible stories for what they say about the meaning of life and how God interacts with history. The individual applies critical thinking skills to figure out the meaning of the story, and many possibilities are examined before the individual chooses the one he thinks most appropriate. Once he has come to this conclusion, he feels confident that he is right.

Simon Peter's experience with the vision of the unclean foods typifies the transition from stage 3 thinking to stage 4. The vision marked a change in policy (as he saw it) from the ultimate church authority, God Himself. Peter at first insisted that in no way would he consider eating the unclean foods. God persisted in offering it to him. He finally gave up his old way of thinking that certain foods and people were unacceptable to God. He had to rely on his own judgment to convince other believers of this change of direction as he had no backup from fellow Christians with whom he associated. Because of his own experience, not just because it could be read in the Old Testament, Peter was able to declare, *I now realize how true it is that God does not show favoritism* (Acts 10:34).

One would not normally encounter a child or young teen in this stage of faith. Not all young adults or even older adults conform to stage 4 thinking; many would identify with stage 3 and some would still relate to stage 2. The person with stage 4 faith thinking would be quite capable of formal operational thought (Piaget) and Kohlberg's stages 4 and 5 moral reasoning. The teacher of college-age young adults would be wise to provide plenty of opportunities for discussion of the meaning of Bible stories. People in this stage of faith long to discover the meaning of God's interaction with humans and what this implies for ethical behavior today.

Stage 5: Conjunctive Faith

Even Fowler admits that he struggles with his understanding of stage 5 faith; yet he believes it exists, although it isn't found as frequently as the previous stages. He compares this stage to looking through a microscope and a wide-angle lens at the same time. The individual can see and understand all the sides to an issue yet might readily admit that she doesn't have the complete answer.

The stage 5 adult (Fowler feels that those who reach this stage do so in mid-life or later) sees benefits in looking for truth outside of her own tradition. She is confident enough in her own beliefs to believe that one can learn from the religious beliefs of others. The symbols and rituals of a variety of others are valid because she can begin to comprehend how meaningful they are to those who hold them dear. Her own traditions have deepened in meaning for her. Faith is much more than an intellectual exercise as it is for many in stage 4; it is a powerful way of looking at life and realizing that the unexpected may be just around the corner.

The mature faith of the apostle Paul might well have been stage 5 faith. Paul seemed not to be threatened by cultures and traditions different from his own. Indeed, he appeared to have welcomed conversing with a variety of people from numerous backgrounds in order to share the Gospel. He was confident of his faith and felt secure enough in it to know when and how to accommodate the message for others without forfeiting his belief system. He realized that he needed training to run the good race. He acknowledged that just as an athlete can continue to improve his physical performance, he never achieved total spiritual maturity and that there was always room for improvement in his faith life. He saw faith as a process that was never complete until death. He realized that he didn't have all the answers, but he relied on God to provide what he needed when necessary.

Stage 6: Universalizing Faith

This final stage of faith is not easily found. People with stage 6 faith see life as it should be and direct all their energies toward achieving that goal. They work regardless of the danger or effect on themselves and sometimes die as a result of their work. They seek to help the oppressed overcome their oppression. Love and justice control their actions in regard to their mission. A stage 5 person might see the mission, whereas a stage 6 person lives for and in the mission.

Fowler believes that this is a level few individuals reach. He suggested Gandhi, the later years of Martin Luther King Jr., Mother Teresa, and Dietrich Bonhoeffer as examples of persons who had achieved this level. (Many Christians will disagree with Fowler.) Not all stage 6 faith thinkers are famous; Fowler and others contend that many live their everyday life in this stage without ever gaining publicity or high honor. These people seem to personify God; they are those who daily remind us by their actions and words how God would have us live. However, it would be a mistake to assume that these individuals are perfect or less sinful than the rest of humanity. All human beings are sinful; all have their own faults with the exception of Jesus alone. Stage 6 individuals have the ability to see the world with God's eyes and then devote themselves to making that vision a reality.

A person with stage 6 faith at times probably will regress to another stage. Indeed, some researchers say that when these individuals' faith is threatened in a manner they cannot deal with, they will even return to the basic trust relationship of a stage 1 believer.

The purest form of stage 6 faith existed in Jesus. He understood God's vision for people and dedicated His life to helping them achieve that vision. He stuck to His mission regardless of the consequences for Himself, even to the point of death on a cross. Pure love guided His every action. He devoted His life to those who were oppressed by sin, and in the end He was destroyed by those He came to save.

Do not be dismayed if you feel you have not reached one of these "higher" stages of faith as defined by Fowler. Remember, no stage is good or bad in itself; the stages constitute different ways of thinking about faith. As such, they relate to how individuals deal with religious "head knowledge" and don't say too much about "heart knowledge." A frequent criticism of Fowler's work is that it is too cognitive (dealing with thinking and the thinking process) and ignores the trust aspect of faith.

Not all faith development researchers agree with Fowler. Let's examine two other ways of looking at the road to spiritual maturity.

WESTERHOFF'S VIEW OF FAITH DEVELOPMENT

John H. Westerhoff III teaches at Duke University Divinity School. He has studied the question of how best to lead children to spiritual maturity and keep them in faith. In his opinion we place too much emphasis on learning about the Bible or the content of religion and do not give enough thought to helping children's faith grow. Westerhoff believes that children need to experience the community of faith instead of just being taught about believing in Jesus in Sunday school or religion class. He says that faith cannot be confused with religion; they are two different concepts. Religion is about the organized church, accepted documents, theology, and moral behavior. Faith, on the other hand, is a personal dynamic; it is a condition of the heart. It cannot be taught; it can only be shared.

Westerhoff's community of faith has four distinct characteristics. First, the community knows what it believes; it has a clear identity.

Second, it must be small enough that the community is meaningful. He asks, how effective is the Christian community in a congregation with more than 300 members? Can close and caring relationships have the opportunity to develop when there are so many people that one cannot know all of them or sometimes even half of them? However, large churches can counter this difficulty by using small groups to achieve intimacy.

Third, the community needs the presence of three generations who interact with each other. The first generation provides the memory that leads the third generation to develop a vision. The second generation is the present that, when combined with vision and memory, becomes the ministry.

Finally, a faith community unites a variety of people with an assortment of gifts. Certain people or gifts cannot be excluded; the faith community is inclusive.

Westerhoff proposes that congregations develop their educational programs around three ideas: *rituals; experiences within the community;* and *actions, or ministry, in the world.* Children need to be included in the worship of the community. Learning the rituals is one way of understanding what their faith is all about. Children need to experience what it means to be Christian. Christian educators need to take advantage of forgiveness opportunities, then tell stories about forgiveness, and finally promote the conceptualization of forgiveness. Last, when children participate in worthwhile ministry programs such as helping the homeless, they learn that faith makes a difference in people's lives and in how they relate to others.

Westerhoff defines faith as an action; it is a way of behaving that includes knowing, being, and willing. Westerhoff identifies four styles of faith. The relationship of these styles can be compared to the growth of a tree. When a tree is young, it has few rings, but it is still a tree. Different kinds of trees grow at their own rate and with their own characteristics, but all trees need a favorable environment in which to grow. As the tree matures, the rings develop. They do this in a sequential manner. Each ring builds upon the previous ring, and every ring is a part of the tree. Let's examine the styles of faith as Westerhoff defines them.

Experienced Faith

The first ring, or style of faith, is called Experienced Faith and exists through early childhood to young adolescence, but it is not limited to children. Children imitate, explore, imagine, test, create, experience, and react. Westerhoff believes that experience is the basis for faith. Just as Erikson proposed the importance of trust in the infant's life, Westerhoff says that perceiving love and care is crucial in the formation of faith. Children need to experience what it means to be Christian through Christians putting their words into action. Of course, this is essential for all believers, not just young children. When Jesus blessed the children, He provided a way for them to experience faith. He didn't talk theology; He gave them an affective encounter with God's love.

Affiliative Faith

Adolescents and adults need to feel that they belong to a community. This gives them a sense of identity. People with Affiliative Faith (and those beyond it) need many opportunities for involvement in jobs that the community needs done. This can include acolyting, singing in the choir, or counting the offering. Like the neighborhood bar in the "Cheers" TV show, everyone knows your name, and it makes a difference that you came. Opportunities for building "heart knowledge" through participation in the arts is also important. Singing, drama, and crafts can all help connect head knowledge to heart knowledge. Another characteristic of Affiliative Faith is authority. Westerhoff explains authority as the story by which actions are judged and inspired. Individuals need to know the story in order to own it in the next style of faith.

If you look at the lifestyle of the early Christians, you will see many of the characteristics of Affiliative Faith. They devoted themselves to the apostles' teaching; they were learning their story and identifying their authority. They came together and shared their possessions. Everyone felt a strong sense of belonging to this community. They praised God with singing and increased their heart knowledge by the way they related to each other. They experienced faith by doing.

Searching Faith

Sometimes in late adolescence, people will move into a Searching Faith, an important step in spiritual maturity. Even though it can be painful, questioning and even doubt should not be avoided. At this time head knowledge "takes on" heart knowledge in the search for personal meaning. To continue to grow, a person must examine the meaning of the community's story and purpose along with ways the community lives their faith. Part of this process is experimentation. People need to learn about the beliefs and traditions of others in order to truly claim their own beliefs. This style of faith also includes the need to commit oneself to others or to a cause. Sometimes this commitment is short-lived before another commitment is made. However, that is how ultimate commitment is learned. People with Searching Faith still have a need to be included in the faith community. The faith community needs to understand and support the search while recognizing that the searcher still needs to feel experienced and affiliative faith.

Prior to the Reformation, Martin Luther serves as an excellent example of Searching Faith. In the midst of a furious storm, in fear for his life, Luther made a commitment to become a monk. This change in plans went against his parents' wishes that he would become a lawyer. He was raised in the church but as a young monk began to question many of its doctrines. He struggled with himself and with God in an effort to find spiritual equilibrium. He scrutinized his faith community's beliefs and the rituals they supported. This search was necessary in order for him to find a faith he could truly accept. In the process his faith grew. It should be noted that Father Staupitz, his mentor, supported his search and cared for Luther throughout his struggle.

Owned Faith

Westerhoff states that Owned Faith is sometimes called conversion. Whether it is dramatic or simple, cognitive or affective, it will always include a change in people's behavior. Owned Faith involves putting our faith in the forefront of our lives, so everyone we encounter might identify us as Christian. To connect our belief system with our daily life is God's plan for all people. This does not mean that the individual has put aside her need to experience faith, her need to feel a part of the community, or even her need to search and question her faith. The three previous styles of faith all continue to be a part of who she is, but now she deals with these needs in new ways.

The apostle Paul had a dramatic conversion experience after which his beliefs and behavior changed drastically. He lived his faith so that it was evident to all he met. He committed his life to telling and showing others what Jesus meant to him.

Some might say that Westerhoff's theories go the opposite extreme of Fowler's. His ideas are heavy on "heart knowledge" but say little about "head knowledge," the knowing side of faith. Some people feel that he bases his faith styles too much on emotions. Many would also question his identification of Owned Faith as the conversion experience. We know that the Holy Spirit plants faith as early as an infant's Baptism. How this happens, we can't explain, but one does not need to be an adult or even a young adolescent capable of making decisions to have saving faith. The heart is turned toward God when the Holy Spirit works faith in that person; that is the conversion experience. It doesn't need to be a conscious emotional decision in which one decides he or she will now live for Jesus.

Numerous Bible verses tell us that faith is God's doing; it is not something we do. Some religious education experts interpret this conversion experience not as the point at which one comes to faith, but as the realization one gradually comes to at which he can say, "This is my faith; this is what I believe."

Whatever problems one might have with Westerhoff's theology, he does present some worthwhile points. For example, no one type of educational program fits every person within a specific age group. Some teenagers are still in the Experienced Faith mode, while others have moved into Affiliative Faith. This idea complements Fowler's research that people of any age can be stages 1, 2, or 3. Westerhoff believes that many adults remain in the affiliative style, which would correspond with Fowler's belief that many Christian denominations encourage stage 3 faith thinking, which emphasizes identity through agreeing with the church authority.

Westerhoff believes that educational programs need to be geared to guide growth from one style of faith to the next. This can happen when role models interact with others in a way that makes evident their faith and the style in which they relate their faith to life. Westerhoff would provide intergenerational activities throughout the sphere of Christian education. He questions the practice of separating children into like age groups for Sunday schools or vacation Bible schools and would encourage adults, teens, and children to interact in small groups. Instead of age groupings, he would arrange people according to interests. We need to ask, however, whether these arrangements would cause us to lose the blessings we accrue when we adjust learning to the needs of individuals of a given age group.

Westerhoff challenges the church to look at their rituals that mark transition periods. Instead of confirming the young adolescent, he suggests a first Communion at first or second grade to welcome children into Affiliative Faith. Then, at the age when a youth is typically confirmed in the church, a new ritual might mark the move into Searching Faith. This might invite the youth to make a covenant with God acknowledging that, while the coming years might bring turmoil, the searcher prays that the Lord would remain at his side even as he struggles with his faith. Then, as one moves toward Owned Faith, the young adult could celebrate the rite of public confirmation.

GILLESPIE'S EXPERIENCE OF FAITH

V. Bailey Gillespie teaches theology at La Sierra University, a Seventh Day Adventist institution in Riverside, California. He supports the view that faith is an experience. It includes not only what one believes, but also one's feelings about these beliefs. The content of faith and the feelings of faith combine to form the action of faith. Our faith grows as we act on the faith we have.

Instead of identifying stages of faith through which a person moves, Gillespie describes seven major faith situations that correspond to different periods of life. He does not attach specific ages to these situations; they are generalizations, and, as always, there are exceptions to the rule. He openly admits that he has not done extensive empirical research; he based the situations he describes on what he has observed. He seeks not to propose new faith stages but to help ministers and religious educators better serve their specific community.

Situation One: Borrowed Faith

A child learns trust during early childhood based on her relationship with her parents. Some experts believe that if a child has a poor relationship with her parents during these early years, she will find it difficult to relate to a caring God in her adult life. Since a child younger than three has not yet developed cognitive thinking skills, she begins to learn attitudes and feelings about faith and the religious experience rather than the content of faith. Because parents are usually the strongest influence on a young child, what they say and do strongly influences the direction a child will go later in life. Parents teach their children about God more by who they are and what they do than by the religious words they might use to describe God. A child experiences faith—the faith of her parents.

What are the implications of Borrowed Faith for educators? Gillespie suggests that activities need to revolve around the young child's age-appropriate needs. Children need to believe they are important to the church, which is achieved by including them in activities and rituals. Through adult education the church can assist parents in helping their children learn to experience God's love, care, and forgiveness. Parent education starting in the prenatal years is essential. Finally, churches and families must consistently do what they say.

Situation Two: Reflected Faith

In middle childhood the child starts to reflect the faith of others he encounters in the faith community. In attempting to make the faith of others his own, he sometimes creates a distorted reflection. (In my own early middle childhood years, I remember hearing the same liturgy week after week. Every Sunday the pastor would say, "Our help is in the name of the Lord." The congregation would respond by singing, "Who made heaven and earth." The pastor's next line—as printed in the hymnal—read, "I said, I will confess my transgressions unto the Lord." My pastor in the 1950s was a rather stern man with a strong voice, and to my way of hearing, he emphasized the words "I said." Every Sunday I would think, We got it wrong again, and Pastor has to repeat it. No wonder he gets so grumpy.)

During middle childhood the individual's feelings about faith often develop as complete trust in God. Hence, the child will pray for help in passing a test or finding his misplaced baseball cards. New experiences and learning excite the child, and he is anxious to learn new things about God. His vivid imagination helps him "jump into" Bible stories. The study of biblical heroes appeals to the preadolescent. Learning the faith community's story is imperative at this time.

To best reach children at this age, religious educators must conscientiously offer activities that demonstrate what it means to have faith and live by that faith. Elementary-aged children must be actively involved in the life of the congregation. Faith modeling needs to be done both by adults who interact with these children and through the telling of the stories of the heroes of faith.

Preteens benefit from problem solving opportunities to prepare for their next stage of life. (It can be difficult for the adult leader to allow them to do this without jumping in with the "right" answer.) Children have a natural sense of wonder at this age; educators and parents can encourage it through prayer and even offhand comments. ("Look at the beauty of this butterfly God created.") Finally, children need to know their history. God told the Old Testament believers to bind His words on their heads and hearts as well as on their children's. Can we do any less?

Situation Three: Personalized Faith

During early adolescence the individual begins questioning and examining her life. She is in the process of finding a faith she can own. Religious experience during adolescence displays a complex personal perception. She doesn't want to hear just about the past or a "pie in the sky" future; she lives in the present and that is where her concerns lie.

The adolescent desires and experiences freedom. Even those subject to the rules of overly strict parents have reasoned that they don't have to agree with those edicts or abide by them. Adolescents need to be trusted with the freedom to make their own decisions in areas that are age-appropriate. The church ought to provide information and discussion forums for teens to make informed choices about music, use of free time, and life goals without heavy-handedness. In the process they might fluctuate between rejection of and commitment to faith, but experiencing tension is necessary for faith to grow and mature. The faith ensued will be personal and meaningful.

Gillespie encourages churches to recognize young teens and thus help build their identity through involvement. Opportunities to build personal relationships among peers and adult role models is essential. Peer ministry is extremely effective at this age. In building a personal faith, teenagers can be invited to keep their eyes on Jesus as they make minor and major decisions in their life. Effective teachers would utilize simulations, voting, roleplaying, and interviewing among other techniques. Learning and telling stories of God and faith are critical if individuals are to personalize their faith.

Situation Four: Established Faith

In later youth, at about 15 to 18 years of age, the believer moves into an Established Faith. The individual is in the process of forming an identity with God through the questioning process. If parts of Personalized Faith no longer "work" for him, he readily forfeits them and moves on to something that will work. Faith has to relate to daily life; only then can he make a commitment to it. He is attracted to theological discussions that help sort through life issues. If the church preaches that God loves unconditionally, then older youth expect the church to love without prerequisites. They want to be accepted the same way and feel they are an important part of the local congregation.

The educational goal of the church in ministering to this age needs to generate an environment where one's faith can become personal and real. Values and attitudes interest the older youth. They want to discover what God (not the organized church) says about sex, drugs, divorce, loneliness, social ministry, and other real issues of life. They want to know how to put their faith in action in the world in which they live. These teens crave spiritual experiences where they encounter God and people who are truly connected to His will in their lives (as opposed to programmed emotional performances). No educator or youth minister can give this faith to another; he or she can only guide them in the process of discovering it for themselves.

Situation Five: Reordered Faith

The young adult of about 18 to 28 years of age often reinterprets her beliefs. She focuses on putting her beliefs into practical use as she takes her place in the world. During this time of life she often deals with doctrinal issues in a cognitive way. Yet the individual wants to feel God's presence in her life as well as intellectually understand her faith. Relationships with others continue to be important. Frequently this experience of faith begins when a major change comes into her life, such as choosing a mate, the birth of a baby, or beginning her professional life.

Although people of this age are drawn to the cognitive aspect of life, educators and ministers need to provide affective experiences along with the intellectual. Problem solving that leads to action enables people to look at themselves and what they are doing in life. Adult learners are introspective; that is, they tend to learn in order to apply the learning to their lives in a practical way. The church must provide experiences, together with rituals or celebrations that recognize typical transitions in the young adult's life.

Situation Six: Reflective Faith

In middle adulthood the individual begins to realize that time is finite. If he is going to do that something he'd always thought he'd do, now is the time to do it. The middle adult years bring the ability to look back, evaluate, and make judgments. Because of this, adults often have opinions that are not easily changed. Middle adults often focus on three areas: the past (to understand how one reached the present), the inside (to understand one's self and grow spiritually), and the beyond (to understand changes that need to be made before it is too late).

Middle-aged adults are capable of personal reflection. This should be encouraged to assist them in understand the meaning of faith in their lives. A retreat that offers time for contemplation is one effective way to do this. Adults want a God who will meet their personal needs. They want to better know and trust God. To grow in faith it is necessary for them to understand their own needs in order to see how God will fulfill those needs.

Situation Seven: Resolute Faith

It was once thought that the life of the older adult, as well as her religious faith, was fixed and somewhat boring. Researchers have discovered that the senior years bring powerful changes and an interesting variety of religious feelings. The older adult bases faith on wisdom that is both cognitive and affective. God comforts the older adult. The past cannot be changed, and looking back, she realizes how God has been at work throughout her life. She puts into perspective what might have seemed immensely important years earlier. Resolute Faith finds hope in a future that is filled with unknowns. This hope brings the motivation of empathetic caring and reaching out to others. Often a sense of fulfillment comes not from reviewing life's achievements but from a deep trust in God.

Ministry to older adults needs to speak to the changes they are experiencing whether it is health, use of leisure time, or life's purpose. The faith of seniors is still in the process of growing, and programs ought to reflect that. Mature adults must be utilized in a variety of ways that will help bring meaning to their lives and the lives of others. This might include intergenerational tutoring, a foster grandparents program, and senior discussion groups. They need to know they are needed. Outlets for sharing their wisdom and reaching out to others with their expertise might need to be provided.

When considering Gillespie's ideas, care must be taken to avoid the trap of thinking that faith is something one does; however, Gillespie himself repeatedly points out that faith is a gift given by God. He proposes offering different experiences to the various stages of life in order to assist the faith of the believer to grow, mature, and develop. Faith involves one's intellect (how he thinks and gives meaning to his life), one's feelings (how he has experienced God in his life), and one's behavior (his response to God's action in his life). Gillespie attempts to reach all of these areas.

Critics might accuse Gillespie of doing no empirical research following the rules of theory development. However, he might argue that his ideas are based on years of observation. Many religious educators concur with his findings. It is up to the reader to decide if faith as experienced holds true in his or her life.

What are the implications of Gillespie's work for religious education? First, educators need to consider the developmental process as they plan their programs. We must determine what teaching techniques and learning activities are best applied at various ages.

Second, we must carefully evaluate age groupings. At certain periods of life, issues and concerns so dominate a person's life that he needs to relate to others dealing with the same issues. At other times, interage groupings are beneficial.

Third, to be effective pastors and teachers ought to understand the needs and characteristics of those they lead and convey a sense of empathy. It's important not only to know the individuals within your care but to be familiar with the developmental research on people of that age.

Finally, religious educators need to take time to explore their own identity and goals. Sometimes we become so focused on the job at hand we forget why we are doing it. Occasionally, the religious educator becomes so intent on teaching that he or she forgets that "who the teacher is, is what the teacher teaches." If we are hoping to teach forgiveness, we must be forgiving. If prayer is the topic, we need to pray with our students and model listening so they can begin to understand how God listens to us and how we need to listen to God. Not to be overlooked, we need to pay attention to our own spiritual needs, and just like Jesus, retreat into the wilderness for personal renewal.

PUTTING IT ALL TOGETHER

We have presented the work of only three experts in the field of religious education. (See the table at the end of this chapter.) There are many others. The insights of these three were not presented because their ideas are infallible; indeed, there are weaknesses in all of them. However, their theories do present food for thought, and they all have some practical application.

I believe that Fowler's work relates to how people respond to the "head knowledge" of their faith and the cognitive processes they go through as they examine what they believe. My faith in not based on rational thought, but I cannot deny that an intellectual side exists. Stages 1 through 4 ring true for my personal experience; I have more trouble understanding stages 5 and 6, which perhaps reveals my own developmental stage.

Westerhoff provides some helpful insights about the setting for religious education. I believe "involvement in" and not just "attendance at" a local congregation does much for building one's faith. His styles of faith do seem to hold true for many Christians; yet they almost seem too simple. I'm not sure they cover the breadth of the faith experience. In addition, Westerhoff says little about the rational side of faith, which we cannot completely ignore.

Although Gillespie's Seventh Day Adventist background is quite different from my Lutheran framework, I find his ideas intriguing. His situations of Borrowed Faith, Reflected Faith, and Personalized Faith seem to describe fairly accurately my childhood faith experiences. Faith was so much a part of my life that I did not question or really examine it until I reached high school. I like how he blends the need for both heart knowledge and head knowledge at each level of maturity. While I agree that middle childhood is a period of needing heroes, I would caution the educator to take care in the way Bible heroes are presented. We must emphasize that God enabled these people to perform great feats and that He used them for His glorious purposes. We don't want to give the impression that these men and women did heroic things on their own because they tried hard and succeeded.

Before you continue with the final chapters of this book, it's your turn. How do you see the road to spiritual maturity or faith development? Can faith best be defined by cognitive stages, community experiences, personal situations, or something else? Which of the theories presented in this chapter are the easiest and hardest for you? Perhaps one way to do this would be to write a list of the pros and cons of each of the theories studied. Which will you apply to your classroom teaching? What difference will they make in the way that you teach?

In the next chapters, we'll look at various age groups and discover how to apply human and faith development theories to each specific age.

Faith Development Theories

Approximate Ages	Fowler's Stages	Westerhoff's Styles	Gillespie's Situations
Infant to Toddler (0–2)	Undifferentiated Faith		
Early Childhood (2–6)	Stage 1: Intuitive-Projective Faith	Experienced Faith	Borrowed Faith
School Years (7–11)	Stage 2: Mythic-Literal Faith		Reflected Faith
Adolescence (12–18)	Stage 3: Synthetic-Conventional Faith	Affiliative Faith	Personalized Faith
Young Adulthood	Stage 4: Individua-tive-Reflective Faith	Searching Faith	Established Faith Reordered Faith
Mid-life and Beyond	Stage 5: Conjunc-tive Faith	Owned Faith	Reflective Faith
	Stage 6: Universal-izing Faith		Resolute Faith

My View of Spiritual Maturity and Faith Development

Chapter 5

Faith of Young Children

*B*efore you read this chapter, review the Publisher's Preface.
*As you design learning experiences, remember that you can provide
the context for faith to begin and grow. Only God can provide the
power for that growth.*

While early childhood is often defined as the period of life from
birth to age eight, this chapter concentrates on the area of growth
between ages two and five. Just the thought of a room full of
preschoolers strikes fear in the hearts of many adults. For others, the
vision of 15 to 20 little ones brings a broad smile to the face. What
is it about these little dynamos of energy that produces such different responses even among well-seasoned teachers?

To say that the average preschooler is a dynamo is no under-
statement. They have a faster heart rate and higher metabolism than
adults. They tire less quickly and have a faster recovery time. They
are not as quick to react to extremes of heat or cold. Young children are active and enjoy moving purely for the thrill it gives.
Because they are always on the go, they need resting times, but they
don't always realize they are tired and need help in relaxing. Most
preschoolers will need an afternoon nap or at least a sustained quiet
time.

Obviously, this is a period of much physical growth. The average four-year-old has reached about 60 percent of his adult height.
While a two-year-old still moves somewhat awkwardly and has little
small motor development, a five-year-old can move in a variety of
ways (jumping, kicking, and possibly skipping) and is able to perform intricate skills.

Socialization is an important aspect of this period of life. A two-year-old will play next to another child and yet appear to ignore him. Her attention is focused on her toy. The concept of sharing is beyond her understanding. If he asks to play with the toy, she usually responds with a definite no! Arguments erupt frequently, but they are quickly forgotten.

By five years, most children will welcome the opportunity to play with other children. They cooperate in playing games and acting out fantasies. Most realize that sharing is an expectation, not an option. The period from two to five is characterized by six different types of play.

* *Unoccupied behavior* results in children either watching other children play or doing aimless activities.
* In *solitary play* children play alone with dissimilar toys while ignoring children playing close by; there is no interaction between the children.
* *Onlooker behavior* causes the child to watch others playing while sometimes making comments about them but without attempting to join the play.
* In *parallel play* children play independently with similar toys beside other children.
* In *associative play* children play with others in a disorganized way with everyone playing by his or her own rules.
* Finally, by the end of this period, most will participate in *cooperative play,* where rules are made and roles (leader, etc.) assigned.

Intellectual growth blossoms during the early childhood years. Two-year-olds are just beginning to learn to express themselves verbally. Three-year-olds possess a vocabulary of about 900 words. By the time they are four, their vocabulary expands to about 1,500 words. Most five-year-olds have at least a 2,000 word vocabulary. While there is great growth in verbal ability, it's important to remember that all preschoolers still think in concrete terms.

Let's take a look at each year in a preschooler's life. Remember, the following scenarios are based on generalities. An "average" composite child presupposes that some children will be more advanced and others will be learning and growing more slowly. Every child develops at her own personal rate. As long as development is occurring, there should be no cause for alarm.

THE TWO-YEAR-OLD

Caitlin is your average two-year-old. She knows her name, the name of her older brother, Jason, her playmate next door, and the name of her baby-sitter. She's learning colors; red is her favorite. Numbers still confuse her, but she knows she is no longer one year old, now she is two. There's a lot she'd like to say, but she often relies on Jason to verbalize her wants and needs for her.

She loves to run, but she still sometimes ends up sitting when she thought she was moving. She is a doer. Jason has set up an obstacle course that includes her small indoor slide, a traffic cone to run around, a chair to crawl under, and a trash can to drop her soft basketball in. She tries to imitate his smooth movements through the course, but duplicating his slam dunk is beyond her ability. She has several simple puzzles, yet Jason can get his more complex ones done faster than she can arrange her easy ones.

When she is tired, Caitlin only wants her mom, and she never likes to be too far out of her sight if Jason isn't around. It's never difficult to judge what kind of mood she is in. When she is happy her face beams, and it's hard not to reflect her sense of joy. On the other hand, when life displeases her, her family (and sometimes all the neighbors) knows it. Play can be serious as she solemnly addresses each new skill she wants to conquer. Yet silliness has a place in her life, and there's nothing sillier than a silly two-year-old!

Mother and daughter participate in a play group that includes five other two-year-olds. There's a noticeable difference between Caitlin and Cyndi, who is eight months older. Caitlin doesn't inter-act much with the other children, other than occasionally trying to take their toys if they look more interesting than what she has. When the six mothers got their inspiration for the play group, they thought it might provide stimulating adult time for them as well. They have since decided to have a monthly Moms Night Out since the play group requires their constant attention. When Caitlin has a problem during play group time, she immediately runs to Mom to solve it. Those other moms are nice ladies, but she goes to her mom.

Caitlin's Christian parents have taught her a simple bedtime prayer and meal prayer that she likes to repeat. She talks about Jesus and agrees that He is her best friend and that He loves her.

She attends church with her family almost every week. Occasionally she responds to the music the Praise Band plays by swaying to it. Even though she sometimes gets noisy, she prefers to stay in church with her family. Taking her to the nursery often results in an angry no!

HINTS FOR TEACHERS OF TWO-YEAR-OLDS

Two-year-olds need to feel unconditional love and acceptance. They need to interact with adults in positive ways. The teacher needs to show interest and concern for the child. This is how young children begin to understand God's love for them. One approach is to talk to them about their mommies and how God loves them so much that He gave them a mommy to hug them, kiss them, tuck them in at night, and do all those things mommies do. Then talk about daddies and what a daddy does. Other names for daddy could be talked about. Explain how God gave them a mommy and daddy and how God is like a mommy and daddy. He loves children very much.

They like copying simple worship as they begin to learn about worship. Learning simple rituals like folding their hands for prayer becomes meaningful to them. Prayers, songs, and hearing Bible stories are learning opportunities, although the process might be more meaningful than the context at this age. They can relate to the idea of family and feel like they're a part of God's family, too. They can learn to recognize the Bible as "God's Book."

Two-year-olds need to be allowed to do things at their own pace. Since they think very literally and concretely, they learn by doing and experiencing things. They need to explore and experiment. Teachers need to encourage children to try things on their own without immediately doing for them. When the results of an activity aren't quite what the teacher desired, the children still need to be praised for trying.

At this age children will not know how to share. This developmental task doesn't come naturally or easily for most. There is a school of thought among many preschool teachers that two- and three-year-olds should never be required to say, "I'm sorry." They cannot conceptualize how another child might feel; they only know how *they* feel. For example, Evan takes Chad's ball. Chad starts to cry. The teacher intervenes by saying, "Evan, you want a ball. (This puts words to Evan's behavior.) Chad wants to play with a ball, too. (This points out to Evan that another child is involved in the situation.) Chad is unhappy. I can tell by his face. I will find you another ball, but this one is Chad's." This plants the seed that someone else was in the picture; gradually they will realize that other people have feelings, too. To force the child to say "I'm sorry" (when they usually aren't) implies that apologizing is the way to get others to leave him alone so he can return to doing what he wants. When "I'm sorry" is spoken from the heart because the child can understand the other person's feelings, it becomes meaningful to all involved in a situation.

Dramatic play with children imitating the teacher's actions appeals to two-year-olds. They like "sound" words. "Jesus' friends threw their nets into the lake to catch fish. Splash! Splash!" The children repeat "Splash! Splash!" "When they pulled the nets up (teacher acts out pulling up a net), the nets were full of fish. Flip flop. Flip flop." (The teacher flip flops her hands, which the children imitate as they say "Flip flop.") They enjoy interacting with the storyteller.

Young children's attention span is limited. Usually about five minutes of listening or quiet time is the most they can handle. Large pictures can capture their attention. They may or may not answer simple questions about a story; they're more likely to respond by pointing to parts of a picture. Activities need to alternate between active and quiet. Transitioning from one to another can require creative teacher thought using songs, stretching, or follow the leader actions. Clapping or marching to music appeals to many. This needs to be demonstrated as many will not yet respond to verbal directions. Remember to keep activities simple and doable for the age; they need to experience success.

Although two-year-olds like activity, they have a long way to go in their small motor development. They are learning how to hold large crayons and "draw" with them. Scribbling or making marks on paper (wall, tables, or whatever is handy) is fun. The goal is not the finished product; it's the process. It's the doing that is appealing. They can be taught how to put stickers on paper, but those stickers will often be taken off as quickly as they are put on. They cannot yet match a sticker to a place it should go in a picture. Once again, they learn by the process, not the end product.

If you use glue activities, it's helpful to put the glue on plastic

93

lids and let the children use cotton swabs to apply it. Some will not like the feel of sticky fingers. Glue sticks can be utilized. The use of scissors is too difficult. Let them tear paper, which is a good tactile experience for them.

The two-year-old's eye-hand coordination is not very well developed. This is due in part to incomplete eye development. Provide large items or pictures for viewing. Avoid the use of books with small print or other small items that could tire their eye muscles.

THE THREE-YEAR-OLD

Raymond has been in preschool for four months now, and he loves it. His vocabulary consists of about 900 words; so although he seems he is always talking, he sometimes has difficulty expressing himself. He is proud to tell what he does know: the colors in the rainbow painted on his bedroom wall, the numbers one to six, and the difference between a circle and a square. He likes talking to his retired next-door neighbors, the Gradys, whom he calls Mr. Grady and Mr. Grady's mother.

He is a very active little boy. After raising her three daughters, Grandma wondered if he was hyperactive, but his teacher has assured the family that he is a normal energetic preschooler. He's grown about three inches in the last year, but his physical development is even more remarkable. He runs, jumps, hops, leaps, and marches. He likes to play catch with Dad even though he still sometimes misses. He can manipulate smaller toys much more easily than he could a year ago.

When he first started preschool, he didn't want Mom to leave, but now he runs to greet his teacher and get his school day started. He knows his teacher loves him and he loves her, too. One thing he likes is the way she lets him try things on his own. He's aware that she is never too far away if he really needs help. When he's overly tired, he likes to crawl onto her lap for reassurance.

He talks to the other children in his class primarily on a one-to-one basis. He and the other three-year-olds engage in parallel play without really interacting with each other. He doesn't usually initiate sharing but is beginning to learn that it is expected. He is still egocentric and has trouble relating to the fact that other people have feelings, too.

Raymond has "Jesus Time" in his preschool class, and he tells the Gradys that God loves him and he loves God. When he accidentally knocked down tiny Libby in the sandbox and she cried and cried, he felt a sense of shame. He didn't mean to run into her, but she had a bloody knee. His teacher told him that Jesus loves and forgives him, and that made him feel better. Raymond likes to pray the snack prayer in a loud voice, but Mom says that voice is too loud to use in church.

TIPS FOR TEACHERS OF THREE-YEAR-OLDS

The teacher of three-year-olds needs to allow them time and space for movement. They learn though the five senses by doing. They need to be allowed to explore and experiment at their own pace. Their eye-hand coordination is improving, but they need opportunities to use it. Their large muscles require frequent use while small muscle control is still developing. Blocks, wagons, small slides, and climbing apparatus are used. Because of the propensity for constant activity, teachers need to provide quiet activities interspersed with more active endeavors.

A stable environment will give the child a sense of security. Unconditional love and acceptance help them accept themselves and encourages their growing sense of autonomy. Although they might not appear anxious to be with other children, they need time to play and talk with youngsters their age. Sharing should be encouraged since this is not a trait that comes easily.

Three-year-olds need opportunities to pray, praise, and sing. They like action songs and acting out Bible stories. As the concept of "friend" is beginning to take root, they respond to the idea that Jesus is their Friend. They understand that the Bible is special. They like feeling that they are part of God's family.

Three-year-olds will spontaneously and confidently express their faith. Sometimes they will say, "Mommy is sick today. I need to tell Jesus." When that occurs, the teacher needs to pray with the child without delay. To put the child off until "prayer time" sends the message that there are only certain times people can talk to Jesus. Some children feel comfortable having the teacher pray for their needs while others will confidently talk to God using their own words.

Read how a three-year-old's faith taught her teacher what it means to trust.

BUILDING FAITH ... ONE CHILD AT A TIME

> Kyra, age three, came to school one day really sad, eyes [filled] with tears, face red from crying. Daddy and Kyra had a "fight" on the way to school, and Kyra didn't get her way. After calming her down, I said, "I'm sorry you are sad. What can I do to make you happy?"
>
> Kyra patted my hand and said, "Let me talk to Jesus!"
>
> I started to say some words in prayer when Kyra put her hand over my mouth and responded, "No, I talk to Jesus ... you listen for me." And with that she "talked" these words: "Please, Jesus, help my daddy not to be mad. I love my daddy. Thanks." She lifted her eyes to me and said, "See, Jesus will take care of that." And she went off to play.

Someone has done an excellent job of modeling faith in prayer for Kyra. Three-year-olds feel comfortable talking to Jesus, although their prayers will be egocentric. They will pray for scratched knees or new bikes, but once again, it's the process that's important. To enable young children to reach this point, start with short echo prayers. Give them time to pray what's in their heart. Although they are just putting their words together to work for them, the more they are allowed to say, the more their vocabulary grows, and the more comfortable they become talking to Jesus.

While three-year-olds still have a short attention span, they will sit in small or large groups to hear a story. They like to have short, simple stories repeated, especially if the story is about "children like them." Finger plays and puppets intrigue them. At this age, they begin to enjoy dress up and acting out the story as the teacher tells it. Three-year-olds sing enthusiastically, even if they aren't quite sure of the words or the melody. They seldom tire of repeating songs, especially if movements go with them.

They begin to answer a teacher's questions, although it's difficult to wait for her to call on them. Sometimes answers will be totally unrelated to the questions, and at other times they will easily answer who, what, and simple questions about the facts of the story. They can comply with one-step directions. Multistep directions will probably confuse them. A gentle touch helps focus them to the teacher's words.

Three-year-olds love artwork. Their creations often look like no more than scribble, but they have a purpose as they produce it. They will tell you about their pictures. When working with stickers, they can place them more accurately than they were previously able. They enjoy gluing activities, but they still need the assistance of a glue stick or a cotton swab. Some begin to learn to use blunt-tipped scissors; there is plenty of time to work on this in the future. Tearing is still developmentally appropriate. When scissors are used, cutting paper into strips is more likely to occur than cutting around an object. It should be noted that although boys are often bigger than girls at this age, the girls are more advanced in almost all other types of development, especially small motor skills. Avoid comparing boys' work to girls' work.

THE FOUR-YEAR-OLD

If Ali is a typical four-year-old, she has now grown to about 60 percent of her adult height. She loves to have her 12-year-old sister, Ami, tell her stories. Her favorite is "Chicken Little." Then she retells the story to her 10-month-old brother, Alan. Of course, he doesn't understand it, but when she throws her hands into the air and shrieks, "The sky is falling! The sky is falling!" they both burst out laughing.

Telling her favorite story is only one way she entertains Alan. She sorts large plastic beads according to color and explains what color each is. In the morning before her parents get Alan out of his crib, she will gallop and whinny like a horse for him. Sometimes she will leap or march from one side of his room to the other. She crawls into his crib and sings songs to him using finger motions.

Ali goes to a preschool operated by her church. When she comes home, she talks about her teachers and Pastor Jim, who stops by the school frequently. She likes to see him in his "pastor dress" on Sunday mornings. She usually goes up front for the children's sermons, although at first she insisted that Ami accompany her. She knows several prayers and is learning to compose her own prayers based on her concerns.

Ali's best friend at preschool is Ellen. Jimmy used to be a good friend, but his family moved to another state. Ali was sad when she realized that he wouldn't be coming back to school. Her teacher helped her write a short note to Jimmy, and she drew a picture for him. Soon after she started talking about her friend Ellen. Their favorite game is playing fire fighters, but sometimes it seems as if they are involved in two different scenarios. The two girls talk and giggle together.

They have about a 1,500 word vocabulary, and they use it!

ADVICE FOR TEACHERS OF FOUR-YEAR-OLDS

Although a four-year-old's attention span is getting longer, it still is short compared to that of older children's. Activities need to be changed frequently. Their thinking is still literal, but they can be challenged to stretch in this area. When sorting objects into sets, they can be asked to explain why they arranged the groups as they did. Manipulation of objects is important to their learning. Even though their vocabulary is growing, they will devise and utilize their own rules of grammar. There will be a wide variety of skill levels within any group of four-year-olds. Allow them to progress at their own rate. They still appreciate repetition. Their humor seems silly to adults.

Teachers need to encourage them to use words to express their feelings and to identify the emotions they feel. In doing so, they will learn that there are right and wrong ways to express their emotions. An attentive teacher is an important factor in their social growth. Listening will inspire them to share their ideas with adults and other children. They still might need some prompting to talk with other children.

Four-year-olds will express their love for Jesus in songs, prayers, and worship. They will make up their own prayers and are able to ask for forgiveness. They want to love and obey God. Teachers need to furnish them with frequent reminders of God's love. Bible stories can be acted out and action songs used. The children will learn that the Bible is God's special word to them. They can recognize that church and worship are different times requiring special behaviors.

Some four-year-olds are ready to predict what will happen next in a story. They can discuss what a story is about and relate it to their own lives. "Jesus loved the little children. He loves and blesses me, too!" Dramatizing stories are an especially effective way to teach them. Some children will feel comfortable being a main character in the story; others can be rocks or trees. They are capable of echo pantomime repeating the teacher's words and actions. Dressing up for their part in the story adds to the fun. Singing remains a pleasing activity. The songs begin to make sense to them, and they can talk about the truths that are found in them.

These preschoolers can begin to answer questions accurately. Some will be able to take turns and even listen to answers that other children give. Two- and three-step directions begin to be followed; however, the teacher must be sure to give directions clearly. Some will still need a teacher's touch to help them focus.

In art activities many four-year-olds will have the end product in mind when they begin to draw. They like to explain the story their pictures tell. Having an adult write the story is important to them. The process of making something doesn't become less important, but the product begins to be important also. Along with that is the desire to have their names written on their work, which is part of their developing sense of identity. The improvement in small motor development often leads to the ability to cut shapes when using scissors, although some will not achieve this until a year or two later. Playing with glue is fun, but the amount of glue they can use should be controlled by pouring it out on plastic lids.

The four-year-old has a developing sense of time and can recognize the passage of time. He is capable of understanding that he has to wait until the late afternoon for Mommy to come home. He likes routines and learns them easily. He knows "what to expect when" if it happens on a regular schedule. When routines are changed, he needs to know it ahead of time.

THE FIVE-YEAR-OLD

Matt started kindergarten this year, and it didn't take too long for him to adjust to his new routine. One of his favorite parts of school is "share time" when he can talk to the whole class about almost anything he wants. He is learning about different occupations; next week his aunt is going to talk about being a dentist. He can't count to 100 yet; to help him learn, "Zero the Hero" visits his classroom every 10 school days. At the dinner table, he enjoys telling his family about his day and what he learned. He is good at retelling stories, and he likes to talk about the pictures in books. He is learning his sounds and letters and can print both his first name and last initial.

Matt's father enjoys playing soccer, and he is following in his father's footsteps. His soccer ball is played with almost every day after school as he practices kicking, dribbling, and trapping the ball. He's excited about joining a soccer team next spring. His small motor development is also improving. He wrapped his mother's birthday gift with a unique touch all his own!

Every night before he climbs into bed, he picks out the clothes he'll wear the next morning (with only a little supervision from his mother). Once he's eaten breakfast, he gets dressed by himself although he still needs help tying his shoelaces. At school, he plays with a group of boys during recess. His teacher says that he is generally happy and sociable.

Matt's grandpa lives with him, and the two are very close. When Grandpa was in the hospital for a week, Matt was dejected and sullen. It helped to talk to his mom about his feelings. He thinks God must be something like Grandpa who is old, seems to know everything, and always has a twinkle in his eye. Matt tells Grandpa stories he makes up, which often include outrageous things that happened at school. Once he accidentally broke a picture frame on Grandpa's dresser. He lied and accused the cat of knocking it over.

Matt loves to make things. He asks questions and listens to the answers. He tries hard to make sense of his world. He is curious about his parents' life before he was born. He describes heaven as "the most wonderful place on earth." He loves making silly rhyming words and realizes some of the words he can rhyme he shouldn't say out loud. When he does the wrong thing, he expects to be punished.

Matt likes his teacher. Maybe he will marry her some day. He can't wait to be a part of the soccer team, and it's fun to be in kindergarten. His class is going to a theater to see a "live production" as his teacher calls it. She has told the children they will have to watch it quietly, but they'll like the story. Matt is looking forward to the trip, and he hopes he can sit by his friends. He's just a little worried about sitting still for a whole hour.

CLUES FOR WORKING WITH FIVE-YEAR-OLDS

Just like younger children, five-year-olds learn by doing. They are in tune with all of their senses. They enjoy trying new skills especially when they are successful. They still need plenty of movement and opportunities to continue to refine small motor development and eye-hand coordination.

Allow kindergartners plenty of time to talk. By now their vocabulary has expanded to about 2,000 words. Some children will naturally seem to be better listeners than others; develop strategies that allow everyone a turn. Some children need coaxing on what to talk about. Allow them to respond to questions like, "What's your favorite story? Can you tell us about it?"

Their attention span is increasing. Their sitting time is longer than it used to be, but once they have reached their limit—that's it! (This generally comes faster for boys than girls.) They enjoy many different types of stories. Reading is associated with the words on the page, and children will often follow along. They will not only retell stories but sometimes memorize them. (Parents will occasionally be fooled into thinking that the child has already learned to read when a favorite book has been memorized.) They will listen to a story and be able to tell about a time they had a similar experience or felt the same way the main character in the story felt.

The five-year-old enjoys meeting new adults and encountering new situations. He is becoming quite self-sufficient and is capable of working without direct supervision. He has better control over his emotions, and emotional outbursts are not as common as they once were. Although he is self-centered to a certain extent, he can be compassionate and understanding. The joys and risks of friendship are becoming apparent to him. He still confuses fantasy with reality and has a vivid imagination.

Spiritually, five-year-olds will express their love for Jesus and identify that He died on the cross. They will say Jesus and God interchangeably. They know that wrongdoings are sins, and because of their cognitive and moral development, they believe that God loves good people and hates bad people. They recognize sin, but like many of us, they see it more readily in others than themselves. They pray their own prayers but more in imitation than felt need. The felt needs they pray about tend to be very concrete and self-centered, "Help me find my cat."

Kindergarten children love to sing and have a repertoire of memorized songs. They will quickly learn new songs, especially those with repeated choruses. Their sense of rhythm is improving as is their response to the tempo of a song. They enjoy making up their own songs and melodies.

Five-year-olds like to answer questions. They are able to listen to the responses of others and reply to their ideas. Group discussions are now possible. However, it is still beyond their reasoning capabilities to transfer learning to new situations. They can follow more detailed directions, but some children will still get confused beyond two or three steps. They are beginning to form a logical system that helps them remember directions.

These children can listen to a Bible story and then draw a picture about it. They will think about their drawing before they begin and plan what they want to include. Although they are still mastering skills, adults will be able to discern what most kindergartners have drawn. They like adding words to their pictures and will use inventive spellings to tell a story. They will also evaluate their work, sometimes becoming so disgusted with unacceptable work that they will crumple it up and throw it away before anyone else sees it.

Are you one of those to whom a roomful of preschoolers seems like a dream come true? You will experience many joys in working with these little ones. And may God bless your energy level!

Religious Behaviors of Early Childhood

	Twos	Threes	Fours	Fives
Prayer	Begin to learn simple prayers, fold hands	Memorize simple prayers, begin to verbalize own prayers	Echo longer prayers, say their own prayers	Fold hands and close eyes, ask for forgiveness
Worship	Listen to worship	Loud in their worship, in own words	Love to sing and copy rituals of worship	Joyfully participate as they are able
Singing	Listen and start to respond to music	Repeat simple songs, enjoy movement	Enthusiastically sing favorite songs	Know many songs, create own melodies
Listening	Will get involved in actions, interact with storyteller	Like repetition, enjoy finger plays and puppets	May predict what's next, begin to relate stories to own life, actions	Can retell Bible stories, enjoy all types of stories
Answering Questions	May not respond, will point to parts of picture	Will respond, might be unrelated	Can handle simple factual responses	Capable of group discussion, *how and why*
Following Directions	Need physical demonstration	One-step, might need touch	Two- or three-step	Some can remember multistep
Drama	Simple actions may be repeated	Act out as narrated, like dressing up	Echo pantomime, will take turns as main characters	Dramatic play with costumes, use drama to remember stories

Implications of Research for Preschoolers

Researcher	Theory	What Does This Mean?
Piaget	Preoperational (not capable of logical thought; egocentric)	Young children need objects to manipulate; not able to understand other point of view
Erikson	2–3 years old: Autonomy vs. Shame and Doubt (want to do things for self, feel shame for failure and self-doubt when not allowed) 4–5 years old: Initiative vs. Guilt (active imagination; take the initiative for activities; guilt follows failure)	Allow them to do age-appropriate tasks; praise the effort, not the final outcome Encourage the use of initiative; praise efforts; freely forgive failure
Kohlberg	Preconventional Morality: Punishment-Obedience Orientation (outcome determines wrongness of action; obey because disobedience brings punishment)	Guide toward understanding that accidents are different than purposeful behavior
Fowler	Intuitive-Projective Faith (parents' behavior reflect what God is like)	Provide unconditional love and acceptance to model God's love; connect the idea of a parent's love with God's love
Westerhoff	Experienced Faith (need to experience God's love through the love of others)	Provide experiences that demonstrate God's love; include children in worship and cross-generational activities
Gillespie	Borrowed Faith (a child experiences the faith of the parents)	Include children in activities; provide Christian experiences, not just words

Chapter 6

Faith of Primary Children

*B*efore you read this chapter, review the Publisher's Preface. *As you design learning experiences, remember that you can provide the context for faith to begin and grow. Only God can provide the power for that growth.*

Take a look at a primary classroom, and you'll see lots of energy. The energy might be one of two kinds: energy released by children when the teacher allows for some noise and movement or energy exerted by children trying to be quiet. (We haven't even considered the teacher's energy as she works trying to keep everyone on task!) Some children will be intent on their work. Others will be twirling their hair, chewing their pencils, or bouncing in their seats. Probably one or two of them could not stay in a seat if their life depended on it!

Most first, second, and third graders have enthusiasm for learning. But a wide range of abilities is apparent in any one group of children. Some have already established a classroom role that could become a lifelong pattern of behavior. With a little observation you will be able to pick out the teacher pleaser, the math whiz, the athlete, the clown, the leader, and the follower. Some of the children have already begun to identify themselves as scholars or strugglers in the area of academics.

The role of the primary teacher can be challenging. Some children are already reading; others guess at the words on a page hoping the pictures provide the necessary clues. Some enjoy independent work; others demand what seems like constant attention. Some are extremely sociable (teachers might feel *too sociable*), while a few labor to make even a few friends.

Let's look at the primary child to see what life is like for a first, second, or third grader. Remember that there are always exceptions to the norms of development and behavior. In addition, some children might repeat a grade and be a whole year older than most of their classmates. Some states or schools allow five-and-a-half-year-olds to start first grade, while other localities stipulate that the first grader must be at least six. Because there are so many levels of development and a lot of overlap at this age, first and second graders will be grouped together.

FIRST AND SECOND GRADERS

Angela has been called Angel since the day Great Grandma took her first look at the tiny newborn and announced, "She's such an angel!" The name stuck, and all the children in her first grade class think her name really is Angel. Although she is smaller than most of her classmates, she is well-coordinated. She's been in gymnastics since her third birthday, and her mother is encouraging her to sign up to do a tumbling routine in her school's talent show. Her printing is meticulous, but she's very slow and precise. Her class's favorite game is dodge ball right now. A few of the children complain that it's not fair—Angel is so small she's harder to hit.

Angel gets high marks in academics and behavior. When working in a group, she is often chosen to be the leader, but she doesn't always insist on getting her way. The one person she doesn't like to work with is Davy, who sits across the row from her. She does her best to follow all the teacher's rules. To her way of thinking, Davy seems to break as many rules as possible during the course of the school day. She likes quiet work time. He is continually tapping his pencil or humming under his breath. Davy has a lot of energy, but recess time often finds him completing work that everyone else finished during class.

Reading is Angel's favorite subject. She visits the library once a week and always takes home several books. Her teacher, Ms. Burton, has told her mother that she is reading above grade level. After she reads a book, she likes to draw a picture and explain what the book was about. She has a collection of 20 Berenstain Bears books. When she was younger, she thought that the bears in the zoo talked to each other like the bears in the books when the zoo closed at night. Now she'll confide, "Of course, the Berenstain Bears are make-believe, but they can teach you how to be a good person."

Angel loves to help her mother and her teacher. At home she sets and clears the table. She is responsible for feeding her cat, Mickie. Helping her sister, Mari, isn't as much fun. Angel has figured out that when Mari gives her a job, she does all the work and Mari talks to her friends on the phone. She loves her older sister and likes to spend time with her, but the 14-year-old complains that Angel pesters her. At school her favorite job is passing out papers. Ms. Burton has had to explain to her that even though she does it very well, other children need a chance to do the job, too.

At Sunday school, Angel is one of the first to volunteer to help Miss Kate, her teacher. Sunday school is fun except that Davy is in her class. Angel knows Jesus died on the cross for her sins, but she has a hard time thinking of the sins she has committed. On the other hand, she can think of lots of sins that Davy is guilty of. She knows God loves everyone yet wonders how He can love a person like Davy. Angel sings in the front row of the Cherub Choir. She likes to go to church as long as she can sit toward the front to see what the pastor is doing. It's hard to listen to the entire sermon, so she usually draws on the back of the bulletin. When she is in church, she likes to draw three crosses on a hill with a sun shining down on them.

TIPS FOR WORKING WITH FIRST
AND SECOND GRADERS

Most first and second grade children are extremely active. If you believe that "Absolute Silence Is Golden," these classrooms are probably not for you. The trick in teaching these young ones is finding a happy medium of noise and student productivity. Children need to be allowed some movement within the confines of not disturbing their classmates. Plan for frequent breaks and organize lessons so that they provide for activity. This can be done by having children move their chairs into a circle or having them put completed papers on a table in the front of the room. The use of finger plays, action songs, rhythm instruments, and roleplaying can accomplish two goals at the same time. The attention span of children in these grades is 10–15 minutes maximum. Plan accordingly!

First and second graders can throw, catch, kick, and skip; some are quite adept at these skills. They are learning to jump rope and play dodge ball and kick ball. Many like tumbling; some are advanced in these exercises. If you include tumbling exercises as part of your routine, check with your administrator first (for liability problems) and be sure to provide a mat and plenty of supervision. Relay games are fun, but monitor team rivalry to curtail those who get too competitive. Sometimes it can be helpful to play a familiar game but announce that the winner (or winners) will be the team(s) that do a good job of showing good sportsmanship and encouraging other players.

Even though six- and seven-year-olds no longer take an afternoon nap, they still tire easily. Provide a rest or quiet period after sessions of strenuous physical activity or difficult intellectual challenges. Story or quiet music time lends itself well to this. Small muscle development such as printing needs continued training, but realize that for some, especially boys, this can be exhausting. Avoid spending too much time on paper and pencil activities. When it's difficult for a child to manipulate a pencil, extended practice can actually have a negative effect on the skill level already attained.

Many primary children have difficulty focusing on small print or objects. Print in large letters and use "big books" as often as possible. Many children have trouble alternating between near and far objects because eye development is not complete. Watch for rubbing the eyes, closing one eye, tilting the head, or extreme blinking. This could indicate problems the parents need to be informed of.

Six- and seven-year-olds are making the transition from Piaget's preoperational thinking to concrete operations. They are gaining the ability to think in their heads what they can do with their hands. They will gradually be able to solve problems by thinking about prior concrete experiences. Some children will still not have made this transition by the end of second grade. All first and second graders need many concrete activities to stimulate their thinking. When groups are used, make them heterogeneous by mixing both high and low abilities within the groups so that children can learn from each other.

First graders can copy and write sentences; by second grade most will advance to producing short two or three sentence paragraphs. Sequencing begins to make sense to them as does cause and effect. They recognize the passage of time as they begin to decipher clocks and talk about the months of the year.

FAITH OF PRIMARY CHILDREN

Primary-aged children have complex ideas about the world and misunderstandings about the way the world operates. They ask a lot of questions in an effort to make sense of it all. They want to understand everything, which is one reason they can be so wonderful to teach. They are motivated to learn. They will also try a teacher's patience with endless questions. The manner in which a teacher responds to their queries conveys a subtle message about the importance of searching for answers. They want brief and easily understood information. They don't want to be rebuffed or ignored. When you don't know the answer to a question, look for the information together.

First and second graders are usually self-sufficient enough to work independently and social enough to enjoy group work for short periods of time. Provide opportunities for each. They need to be liked and accepted by their peers. Some children struggle with making and keeping friends. They might need assistance by having the teacher assign partners or teams. Many teachers avoid letting children choose teams or groups since often one or two are always the last ones picked. If you do like to have children choose teams, then allow the last ones picked one day to be team captains the next day.

At this age children need to learn negotiation, discuss their differences, and compromise by evaluating a variety of ideas. Encourage them to verbalize their feelings and tell what they think others might be feeling. Structure activities where they can practice these social skills.

Rules are absolute to most first graders. When someone breaks a rule, they see it as their duty to report the lawbreaker. "Tattling" is almost considered a moral obligation. Children will normally obey rules and directions without question purely because they are the rules. They do not need to have the rationale for rules explained to them. This is convenient for the teacher until she wants to alter a rule for a specific situation. Then there can be resistance and unrest. Primary children still like routines and knowing what to expect.

Design activities for success. Young children need recognition both for their efforts and their achievements. Because they often idolize their teachers, they can be devastated by criticism or indifference. Erikson classified this age as Industry vs. Inferiority. To grow toward positive self-esteem and self-confidence, they need praise and acknowledgment and an assortment of opportunities to produce a variety of projects. They need to know the high status God gives them as His children.

Small motor development has improved to the point that most can cut accurately with scissors and use glue or paste. When drawing people, they will include facial expressions. Their pictures show size relationships. They happily explain the artwork they have produced.

First graders trust God as they trust the adults in their lives. They talk about God as their Father and Jesus as God's Son, but they still confuse God and Jesus. Second graders begin to understand the difference between God the Father and Jesus; some add the concept of the Holy Spirit to their base of knowledge.

Children in both grades express their love for Jesus and know that He died on the cross to forgive their sins. However, they often have trouble identifying the sin in their own lives and lack true repentance. They consider actions to be wrong only when punished. If an act fails to result in punishment, it must not be wrong. When asked about appropriate punishments, some will favor the more severe punishment as this fits their sense of right and wrong. They see punishment as "paying" for the wrong. Because they think in concrete terms and not abstract, they can apply the "letter of the law" but not the "spirit of the law." Therefore, we focus on simple, clear messages from God's Word, messages that do not require complex thought.

According to James Fowler, who examined how people think about their faith, some first graders will be making the transition from stage 1 to stage 2 faith; others (but not all) make this move in second grade. Stage 2 faith is characterized by the need for fairness. Children often understand the God who punishes sin more than the God who forgives sin. We need to exert special effort through words and actions to make His forgiveness real to them. These children cannot yet give meaning to the symbols of faith. They understand Bible stories very literally. Have them retell the stories you share with them to explain any misunderstandings they may have.

John Westerhoff places children up to about age 12 in the category of Experienced Faith. As children are concrete learners, they need to experience faith by putting words into actions and interacting with Christian adults. Don't just talk about the power of God's love; find ways to express it so they experience it. Devise means by which they can put their love into action.

V. Bailey Gillespie would say that the primary child moves from Borrowed Faith to Reflected Faith. This might happen anytime between first and third grades or even later. In Reflected Faith the child begins to develop complete trust in God. Perhaps this occurs in the transition from first to second grade. First graders love to ask questions about God. Second graders are more likely to accept adult explanations without questioning them.

Six- and seven-year-olds will pray aloud in group settings. First graders are more egocentric than second graders. Older children will often pray for others first and then pray for themselves. Children of both grades enjoy "popcorn" prayer in which children pray spontaneously. Although they have trouble recognizing their own sinfulness, when they do see their sin they will pray for forgiveness and ask others to forgive them. They need to hear that they are forgiven for their wrongs. "Jesus forgives you and so do I" are words the children need to hear frequently. They will pray for those who don't know Jesus, especially for those who are family members. They need to experience God's unconditional love through their parents and teachers. They like to talk about things that bother them.

Some first graders will volunteer to read aloud, but they still need to work on fluency. They like listening to stories they are able to read for themselves. Provide opportunities for them to retell stories and relate them to their own lives. Second graders can handle more details from the Bible. They tend to make their faith more personal. They will discuss a story and then use the discussion to build concepts gleaned from the story. First graders have not outgrown getting involved in actions. Drama and puppets can be utilized to teach stories.

Remember that children need to experience God's love, not just to hear about it. When the teacher accepts them without judging them, they experience God's grace. When they need correction and it is done with love and forgiveness, they learn how Jesus loves them in spite of their sins. They will follow the teacher's lead in worship, prayer, and praise. The Christian classroom demonstrates what it means to be part of God's family.

THE THIRD GRADER

At the beginning of third grade, Scott was a little apprehensive about having his first male teacher. His family consists of just his mother and himself, and he hadn't had many opportunities to relate to men. But after the first month, he announced, "Men teachers are just as good as women teachers. They just talk louder." Mr. Riley shoots baskets with the boys at recess, and Scott no longer avoids the basketball courts. He still enjoys playing chase games with a group of boys and girls, but he also feels confident enough to join the more athletic boys practicing their shooting skills. He used to enjoy Miss Marlow's hugs; now he feels that Mr. Riley's habit of putting a hand on his shoulder is much more grown-up.

Scott doesn't feel very smart, but he does enjoy learning. He has trouble sitting for long periods unlike some of the girls in the class. He loves dinosaurs and has memorized names and characteristics of the various species. When his teacher comments on what a remarkable memory he has for scientific data, he beams with pride. His social studies project on the Plains Indians wasn't the neatest or best in the class, but he invested many hours of work in making the diorama and writing his report. He was angry when he couldn't get the tepee to look like the one in his book. Both his mom and his teacher assured him that they were proud of the effort he put into it. He doesn't volunteer to read aloud much, but he will read when Mr. Riley asks him to.

He's definitely not the loudest or most outgoing boy in the third grade room, but he makes up for it at home. Mom picks him up from day care at 5:30; the drive home is spent talking about his day. He knows Mom is usually tired and often worried about money so he tries not to upset her. Over dinner he likes to tell her imaginative stories about the neighbor's dog. Scott would really like to have a dog of his own, but Mom says they don't have time or money for a dog. He is thankful his neighbors let him play with their dog, Heinz. Mr. Garcia says that Heinz has 57 different kinds of dog in him. Scott doesn't care, because Heinz always acts like Scott is his best friend.

Scott loves his mother and worries about her. Even when she says that she's thankful she can send him to a Christian school, he feels guilty about the money she spends on tuition and day care. He prays for his mother every night and asks God to give her money so she doesn't have to worry. Once his friend Nate asked him if he thought she would get married again. The idea troubles Scott whenever he thinks about it. He knows it would probably make her happy, but where would that leave him? Last summer she dated a man named Kevin. When Kevin invited him to a baseball game, he shouted, "You're not my father. I hate you!" When Kevin stopped by their home a few days later, Scott apologized. He had made his mother cry, and he really didn't hate Kevin. Kevin said that he forgave him and the three of them went out for ice cream. Scott felt confused. He expected Kevin to yell at him for making his mother unhappy.

Scott and his mother attend church almost every Sunday. Scott received his own Bible for his eighth birthday, and he likes to read from it if Mom helps him with the big words. He is interested in learning more about God. Last week he drew a picture of a flashlight shining in the darkness. Under the picture he had written, "Jesus is the lite." He explained to his mom that he liked this idea of Jesus, because when he was younger he was afraid of the dark. We see that the Holy Spirit has acted through His Word to build Scott's faith!

When Mr. Riley announced that their class was going to learn about Indians living in Canada where it's very cold, Scott's ears perked up. His grandparents had recently vacationed there and sent him postcards from their travels. Mr. Riley explained that the class was going to collect money to send missionary pilots to Indians who lived so far north that most never had seen a big city. Scott decided that he would give some of the money he earned from collecting soda cans. He couldn't wait to tell his mom when she got off work.

TEACHING THE THIRD GRADER

The third grade year is a transition year. Third graders are in the process of leaving the primary life behind and becoming "real elementary" children. For some this is a difficult transition to make. Many children are ready for the passage to middle childhood, but their parents, fearful of losing their babies, refuse to accept the inevitable. Hence, the third grade teacher often becomes the child's teacher and the parents' coach.

Although the third grader has a longer attention span than most first or second graders, he still needs to move on to something new about every 15 minutes. Third graders often choose to play noisy, active games. Although they enjoy team activities, they haven't outgrown the fun of unstructured play. Because they have improved immensely in the control they have over their bodies in the last several years, they have abundant self-confidence in their physical abilities. Teachers need to be aware that they can be overconfident and even daring in their physical endeavors; the third grade year is a peak year for playground accidents.

While third graders are still attached to their teachers, they are beginning to distance themselves from needing his or her constant approval. This usually happens sooner for boys than girls. Some begin to figure out that having their teacher not like them all the time isn't the worst thing in the world. Yet most third graders would still honestly answer that they like their teachers. Teacher reinforcement is important to them. They need to know they are doing things correctly and will frequently ask, "Is this okay?"

Some third graders begin to get moody and experience ups and downs that seem to fluctuate day-to-day. Friendships that seemed strong one day might disappear the next. However, they need to feel they are part of a group. A child who ostracizes another child one day would complain loudly the next if she were the one who was not accepted. The eight- or nine-year-old is developing more sensitivity to the feelings of other children. Yet sometimes they may use this ability to ambush another child's weakness.

Third graders differentiate between the sexes. Girls often want to play only with girls and boys only with boys, although chasing each other is acceptable. Even sitting next to a child of the opposite sex can be difficult for some. On the other hand, there might be a few who already talk about having boyfriends or girlfriends.

Third graders have a love of trivia. They enjoy quiz show games with a competitive edge; however, the challenge for the teacher is to keep the game from becoming too competitive. While we do not want to give the impression that Bible trivia is the goal of faith, use of this interest can motivate these children to examine God's Word. In so doing, the Holy Spirit has another opportunity to cause their faith to grow.

These children enjoy projects and working in groups. In every class, there seems to be one or two children who do not do well with group assignments. If they prefer, allow them to work independently while others work cooperatively.

These children are still developing their problem-solving skills. Give them opportunities to practice these abilities whether it is in the area of organizing a class party or working out differences with a classmate. When you must intervene in a student problem, allow them to verbalize their feelings about the situation. The teacher doesn't have to agree with them, but they want to be heard.

Eight-year-olds love dramatic productions. This can be a wonderful way to teach Bible stories. Shyer children enjoy being "stage hands" by turning lights on and off or assembling props. Some third graders may begin to write their own scripts and will ask if they can perform them for the class. Each of these activities provides another setting for the Spirit to work faith.

Third graders have a wide range of biblical information and spiritual growth depending on their home situations. With their love of information, some children might possess almost as much Bible knowledge as the teacher. For others, you might be their first introduction to God and His love in Jesus.

Fowler would place most third graders in stage 2 faith; however, some will still possess stage 1 faith. The third grader's basic lament about life is "it's not fair." They see God as a God of fairness who punishes the sinner and rewards those who are faithful. Eight- and nine-year-old children often have difficulty identifying their sins. When they do realize they have done something wrong, they tend to be very contrite and ask for forgiveness. They often expect to be punished to "pay" for their sin.

Westerhoff proposes giving children many opportunities to experience their faith. Since third graders enjoy learning about different cultures this might include mission projects. They also enjoy being with people. Adopting "grandparents" can be an excellent choice for this age. Westerhoff believes that it is essential to involve them in congregational worship and service. Gillespie would suggest providing third graders with many stories of Bible heroes. He recommends building on their natural sense of wonder to see God at work in the world. Games and contests can be used to motivate them to memorize books of the Bible and Bible verses. He also advocates involving the child in the ministry of the congregation and with congregational "faith heroes." God's love becomes evident to the child who sees how God has worked in the lives of these "heroes."

As children begin to develop their thinking skills, they start to understand comparisons. "Jesus is like a light because ..." They enjoy talking about these ideas and then drawing pictures that reflect their perceptions.

Third graders ought to have access to Bibles and learn how to look up specific passages. They need opportunities to read from the Bible itself. Encourage them to read their Bibles at home with their families, too.

Model prayer so they feel comfortable praying aloud. Don't limit prayer time to just one or two specific times during your class. Pray as the need arises. Silent prayer, group prayer, memorized prayers, and popcorn prayers can all be utilized to make children aware of the variety of ways we can talk to God. Some classes pick a "prayer person of the day" program in which all other children are encouraged to pray for that person. Some schools match younger and older children as prayer partners who meet once a week and pray together.

Teachers of all ages have opportunities to share God's love in very personal ways. In addition to sharing God's message, we have occasions through our classroom interactions to show who God is and how God loves us. What exciting opportunities God has given us as teachers!

Religious Behaviors for Primary Children

	First Graders	Second Graders	Third Graders
Prayer	Talk to God in their own words; memorize prayers; popcorn prayers	Confess their sins; popcorn prayers; memorize longer prayers	Listen to liturgical prayers; lead classroom prayers
Worship	Participate in litanies; choose songs; listen to devotional reading	Read from Bible and choose songs that "match"; participate in formal worship	Lead classroom devotions; identify different parts of liturgical worship
Memorization	Short Bible verses, songs; needs to be meaningful	Can memorize longer selections such as Apostles' Creed with repetition	Longer Bible verses, songs, Ten Commandments and meanings
Drama	Action poems and songs; acting out stories	Acting out stories, roleplaying	Drama with props and costumes, roleplaying
Singing	Will sing a variety of songs; action songs; use rhythm instruments	May feel actions and rhythm instruments are too childish; learn traditional hymns; autoharp	Learn to play the recorder and accompany singing; strong sense of rhythm

Implications of Research for Primary Students

Researcher	Theory	What Does This Mean?
Piaget	Preoperational transition to cognitive operational thinking (cannot use logic to solve simple logic-based tasks)	Literal thinking; use concrete objects; cannot understand symbolism; moves from egocentric to relating to others' feelings
Erikson	Industry vs. Inferiority (want to learn and produce; fight feelings that work is not good enough)	Provide tasks that can be successfully completed; give recognition for effort as well as achievements
Kohlberg	Preconventional Morality (physical consequences determine whether an action is right or wrong; obedience should have rewards)	Children might not be able to apply moral principles to new situations (Further research shows that moral knowledge doesn't necessarily lead to moral behavior)
Fowler	Mythic-Literal Faith (importance of fairness, literal interpretation of Bible, moralistic)	Children respond to stories of Law and don't always understand Gospel; do not understand symbolism; need guidance in seeing and admitting their sins; will blame self when bad things happen
Westerhoff	Experienced Faith (need to experience Christianity, not just have it explained)	Provide affective experiences to feel God's love; practice ministry to others
Gillespie	Reflected Faith (attempt to make the faith of others one's own)	Misconceptions need to be explained; faith activities need to be experienced; learn the story of faith

Faith of Elementary Children

*B*efore you read this chapter, review the Publisher's Preface.
As you design learning experiences, remember that you can pro-
vide the context for faith to begin and grow. Only God can provide
the power for that growth.

We often refer to grades four, five, and six as the elementary
years. Students in these grades are usually 9–12 years old, which is
the period some call the preteen years. Children of this age like to
keep busy. The organized, motivating teacher directs their energy
into worthwhile projects. When this energy isn't tapped into interesting endeavors, chaos can rule.

While most 8-year-olds have a love of learning, many 11-year-
olds consider school, or at least certain subjects, boring. Students
who struggle with academics may make fun of their more able classmates and label them "nerds." Some students are no longer concerned that the teacher likes them. Pleasing an authority figure has
fallen in importance to pleasing oneself and one's peers. Sometimes
intentionally irritating the teacher is the criteria for peer esteem.

By fourth grade, most children are quite aware of male-female
differences, and some are already fascinated by these distinctions.
Girls are growing at a different rate than boys. It's not unusual for
preteen girls to be taller and heavier than preteen boys. Some of the
girls have already hit puberty, which often reduces the boys to hys-
terics and bathroom jokes. Girls will look at these immature boys
with disdain and pass notes complaining about them. At the same
time, the girls begin to get more interested in the opposite sex and
pass notes with a simple message to the favored few. The message
often reads, "Check *yes* if you like me, *no* if you don't."

How does an adult best relate to the elementary-aged student? How can a teacher build a positive relationship and yet still clearly be in charge? What can a teacher expect of these preteens anyway? They seem like such a contradiction in terms. What is typical preteen behavior, and how does a teacher deal with inconsistencies?

THE FOURTH GRADER

Jonna came home from her first day of fourth grade with a pout on her lips and a strategic tear rolling past her freckles. "Mom," she begged, "call Mrs. Folsom and tell her to move me into the other class." After some discussion as to why a phone call to the principal might be necessary, Mom finally figured out the problem. Jonna had been best friends with Carrie all through third grade. Now Carrie was in the other fourth grade class, and she chose to eat lunch with Brittney instead of Jonna. Jonna admitted that she had originally wanted to be in Mr. Street's class, but now that didn't seem so important. What she really wanted was not to lose her best friend.

By mid-November, Jonna had adjusted to being in a different class than Carrie. They still played together both during and after school, but Jonna realized she also enjoys the company of Nikki. Jonna, Nikki, Carrie, Brittney, and Laura all play on the same softball team. They spend the night at each others' homes and giggle late into the night. One night Brittney confided that her mom had bought her a bra. Jonna went home the next day and asked her mother if she could have a bra, too. Her mom valiantly stifled her laughter and asked the nine-year-old to write down all the reasons she wanted a bra. Jonna listed: (1) Brittney wears a bra. She stared at her paper for about 10 minutes and then crumpled it up and threw it away.

Although Jonna is slender, she is one of the tallest students in the class. She hates it when the boys call her "Stringbean." In the 4A vs. 4B softball game, she hit a grand slam home run; now some of the kids call her "Slugger."

Jonna's biggest challenge this year has been learning long multiplication. There are a few facts that simply elude her. When Mr. Street announced that no calculators were allowed unless he handed them out, she felt he was being unfair. After all, her father worked with a calculator all the time, and he got paid for it. But even her dad agreed with Mr. Street. He said she had to learn to do the work on her own before she could rely on a machine to do it for her. She's been working on the math, but she still got a C+ on her report card.

Jonna enjoys going to church, but lately she complains about Sunday school. "Miss Nelson treats us like babies!" When asked how she'd like Sunday school to change, Jonna put a lot of thought into it and wrote a list of "Ways to Improve SS": (1) Read new Bible stories, not the same ones we've always done. (2) Don't treat us like kindergartners. (3) Do harder art projects. (4) The teacher should listen as much as she talks.

TEACHING FOURTH GRADERS

By fourth grade, most children's attention span can carry them through 20 minutes of work, or even 30 if the topic interests them. In the past there seemed to be gender differences in specific abilities. Girls appeared to do better in verbal fluency, spelling, reading, and math computation. Boys seemed better in mathematical reasoning and understanding spatial relationships. However, more recent testing indicates that this discrepancy between boys and girls may be diminishing.

A variety of thinking styles becomes evident by this age if not sooner. People tend to gravitate to either characteristic in the following sets. Notice how the pairs are opposites. Most people are a blending of the two characteristics, yet one trait will dominate to determine their particular thinking style:

1. Some children are reflective; they like to consider possible answers before they give a correct response. Other students are more impulsive. They tend to blurt out the first answer they think of. Being quick is more important than being right.

2. Some students are analytic. They pay attention to details and like specific answers. Others are more thematic. They get the "big picture," but details escape them.

3. Some learners can identify the many different parts of a situation or problem. In an argument during a game, they will be able to explain the role various individuals played in the problem. Other children can see only one part of the

whole at a time. In discussing a dilemma in a reading story, they will look at the effect of one character's actions while ignoring how other characters impacted the situation.

4. Some people are able to focus their attention on a project and not allow distractions to sidetrack them. Others are easily distracted not just by physical diversions but mental ones as well.

5. There are those who resist change that is unexpected even when evidence seems to lead in a new direction. Others are highly flexible and open to new ideas.

6. Some students always look for the one right answer, the one way that others expect them to respond. Other students prefer coming up with unexpected responses to stimuli. They enjoy being nonconformists.

These variations in thinking styles should help teachers realize that some students are not necessarily trying to be disruptive or attention-getters; they just might operate on a wavelength all their own. The challenge is to find ways to harness these diverse thinking styles and channel them in positive directions.

Fourth graders do not develop new ways of thinking; they enjoy learning new knowledge using established learning patterns. They like to increase their base of facts in numerous areas. Impressing others with their intelligence is fun. It's even more fun if you know more than the teacher on an obscure topic. Fourth graders enjoy class discussions and are usually anxious to share their opinions. Working on extended projects that require research appeals to them. Most enjoy building models or making displays to share their learning.

Ten-year-olds have a strong sense of right and wrong, but that doesn't make them unwilling to try new and sometimes risky behavior. As peers become more important, this can lead to problems. A fourth grader is not too young to experiment with drugs or other at-risk behavior. The advantage of the age is that other 10-year-olds will often report these actions to adults. As they get older, this becomes less likely. If a student reports a peer's dangerous behavior or attitude, don't hesitate to intervene for the child's sake. Behavioral and academic problems that lead to delinquency behavior are often identified in the middle grades.

Fourth graders are aware of community, national, and international problems. They may worry about such things as nuclear war or being kidnapped. Most can already identify stress in their lives (busy schedules, expectation of good grades, family problems) but don't know techniques for managing these pressures. They are usually willing to talk about their problems and will seek advice from trusted adults. (I once had a very serious fourth grade boy ask me how to get a girlfriend.) Class meetings work well at this age. Although children at this age are adept at discussing moral behavior, their actions often fail to live up to their words.

Nine- and 10-year-olds are sensitive to the criticism of adults and peers, and they need positive, caring adults in their lives. They no longer want to be treated like little children but will exhibit childish behavior at times. Because they can be easily discouraged when faced with failure, they need much encouragement and praise. The praise given to elementary-aged children needs to be honest and appropriate; they know when they're getting a snow job and will discount it.

Some fourth grade girls have already begun their sexual development. The average age of puberty for girls in the United States is 11; however, it can begin as early as age 8. This can be met with embarrassment, pride, confusion, or all of the above. Naturally, both boys and girls have questions about the changes that some of their peers are experiencing. Be sure to check with your administrator on your church or school's policy regarding sex education before questions or problems arise so you know how to handle them. But in what better educational setting than Christian education can we honestly answer questions and rejoice that we are wonderfully made creations of our heavenly Father?

Most fourth graders are in Fowler's second stage of faith, Mythic-Literal Faith. The 10-year-old looks at the world literally and concretely. Shown a picture of an inmate praying inside a jail cell, some fourth graders might say that he is praying for forgiveness; however, the majority are more likely to say that he is praying to get out of jail.

A 10-year-old's style of faith according to Westerhoff is Experienced Faith. Opportunities to live out their faith is important to fourth graders. They enjoy getting involved in projects and activities. Making greeting cards for shut-ins or decorating tray mats for hospital patients

allows them to share God's good news with others. They like helping others and are usually not too self-conscious to do so.

Gillespie would say that a fourth grader has Reflected Faith. The
10-year-old's understanding of God has deepened since he was an
8-year-old. He has a better concept of the passage of time and so
is able to study the Bible chronologically. Children of this age love
to add to their base of knowledge and appreciate learning some of
the more obscure Bible stories that were not taught in primary
grades. Teachers need to direct students to finding the promise of
God in Christ Jesus in each story. Bible heroes are captivating to this
age, especially when it's a new story about an "old" hero or a brand
new hero that is being introduced to the student.

Although 10-year-olds still have a need for fairness in their lives,
they become better able to grasp the concept of Law and Gospel.
They like to identify ways God works in people's lives today and can
apply basic Law and Gospel concepts to national and local news stories. They are better able to see their own sin than they were in
third grade. Because of this, forgiveness becomes more meaningful.

Many fourth graders are motivated to read the Bible on their
own. Some teachers design at least part of the Bible time for silent
Bible reading for both students and teacher. Others assist students
in organizing a plan of their own on their own time. It's helpful
for students to choose a book of the Bible they'd like to read (a
short one that lends itself to success is best) and divide it into
manageable sections. The children need to hear that everyone
gets distracted from this goal at times and that failing to meet a
Bible reading goal doesn't make them a failure. It's just an opportunity to do it again!

Meaningful worship is important to fourth graders. When congregations offer children's sermons, they often see themselves as
too old for that message. They enjoy preparing and leading classroom devotions and prayers. They are aware of those who don't
know Jesus, and they will demonstrate concern for their salvation.
They are eager to learn ways they can comfortably share their faith
with others.

THE FIFTH AND SIXTH GRADER

A 12-year-old, Tay is consumed by his interest in sports. He
plays football, basketball, and baseball. He likes basketball the best

and hopes to play professionally one day for the Chicago Bulls like his idol Michael Jordan. If his parents let him, he'd watch every professional game shown on television. It's important to him to have the right shoes, and his two-income family can afford to give him what he thinks he needs. His parents have noticed that he's eating more these days; they expect he'll experience a growth spurt soon. His appetite keeps him constantly munching.

Tay moves smoothly on and off the court; his phone rings frequently with girls wanting to talk to him. He's starting to take a little more time in combing his hair in the morning. This results in his 15-year-old sister, Jaqui, teasing him and his 17-year-old brother, Will, giving him advice on "women."

Tay gets good grades. He knows they could probably be a little better but asks, "Who wants to spend all their time studying?" He has the stats of his favorite basketball player memorized and with his friends likes to debate about the best team in the NBA. Math and science are his favorite subjects. Tay hates reading class and once suggested to his teacher that they throw away the book and use *Sports Illustrated.*

He likes to hang out and fool around with his friends. Their science teacher is a stickler for rules, and the boys often ridicule him when his back is turned. However, when Tay's friend Josh broke a beaker clowning around and had to have stitches, he began to see that there was a reason for all of Mr. Hansen's rules. Mr. Hansen has promised that if they have two weeks of good behavior, he'll bring his two-foot-long pet iguana to class. Tay has been reading up on this reptile, and he's encouraging his friends to behave themselves.

Tay would say that he is usually happy, although he hates it when he has a bad game. Even if no one else says anything, he feels it must be his fault if his team loses. He has high expectations of himself and sometimes worries that he won't be the athlete Will is. He loves his parents but thinks they are overprotective since he is the baby of the family. He has good rapport with all of his coaches, and all of his teachers honestly say they enjoy having Tay in class.

Tay's church offers a fifth and sixth grade youth group, which he attends. They usually have an activity like roller blading or miniature golf and then gather for a short Bible study. Tay is interested in talking about God and understanding the pastor's sermons. He believes the Bible is God's true Word to him and wonders about differences in other Christian denominations. In the back of his mind floats the thought that if he can't make it in professional sports, perhaps he'll be a pastor.

HINTS FOR WORKING WITH FIFTH AND SIXTH GRADERS

In my 23 years of being an educator, I've heard more fifth grade teachers rave about the advantages of teaching at their grade level. Fifth graders are independent and can handle a certain amount of freedom when the rules are clearly laid out. They still seem to possess a natural curiosity about many aspects of life and will pursue information for the sake of gaining knowledge. Their sense of humor is developing, and they appreciate a teacher who uses humor to teach.

Sixth graders, on the other hand, can be a little tricky. Educators don't always agree on what makes the sixth grader tick. In some communities, the public elementary school includes kindergarten through grade six. In other places, sixth grade has been moved to the middle school with seventh and eighth grades. Observe carefully the sixth graders you teach. Do they resemble fifth graders? (Oh, lucky you!) Or are they blasting into adolescence like a nuclear-powered submarine? (You have our prayers.) Or, if your sixth grade experience is typical, you probably have some of each. (At least you have plenty of company!)

Eleven- and 12-year-olds undergo bone and muscle growth. Girls have usually hit a growth spurt; the boys will soon follow. Once the boys hit their growth spurt, they have greater strength and endurance than the girls. The students who grow early will probably feel self-conscious and awkward while the smallest ones in the class wonder what's wrong with them. They sometimes become the target for their classmates' jokes. Teachers need to calm the inner turmoil their students experience by explaining that eventually everybody ends up about the same anyway. Because of the impending growth, they might tire more easily than when they were in fourth grade.

The preteen's small motor coordination enables her to do many activities she could not manage just a few years ago. Arts and crafts are popular pastimes. This is the age many begin to excel in playing musical instruments. Although many students are interested in playing sports, parents and other adults need to remember that bone growth isn't complete, and caution still needs to be taken. Fifth and sixth graders have lots of energy. Some still have trouble sitting for long periods of time. Their energy level and corresponding increased activity leads to an increased appetite.

Friends are important to both fifth and sixth graders. For some the peer group has become more important than parents, teachers, or other adults in influencing behavior. Passing notes in class is common at this age, and students, especially the girls, devise creative postal systems to send a note across the room undetected. The mail system seems to be most active either among the best of friends or the worst enemies; there's seldom middle ground here. Most students make friends easily. Those who don't and act like they want friends might need some teacher intervention.

Although preteens are not as attached to their parents as they used to be, they still need positive adult role models. Coaches, club leaders, and preteen youth leaders can all serve this function.

By age 10, most children realize that what a person says is not necessarily what he feels. By age 12, many can analyze their own behavior and feelings as well as the behavior and feelings of others. This allows them better to deal with social problems. They are more open-minded about other people's feelings, and they are more able to change their attitudes and behavior because of this.

Many things create emotional stress in the life of a preteen. Being rejected by one's peers, family problems, and low academic achievement all lead to low self-esteem. Children with low self-esteem often bond with others in the same predicament. They often find they can receive the attention and recognition they crave through negative behavior. Sometimes adults assume that they will outgrow this problem, but all too frequently, the stage is set for a troubled adolescence. While it is never too late to help a struggling youth, now is the time to take an active role in making a difference in a child's life, before the debris thickens into quicksand.

Every preteen needs to excel in something whether it is an area of academics, sports, music, scouting, or service. Some schools take at-risk students and match them with service activities: office aides, primary teacher aides, computer assistants, etc. These programs match students with positive adult role models and provide opportunities for them to help others in a positive context. Students with low academic achievement tutor younger students; they then realize how much they've learned and are often motivated to continue learning.

Current studies reveal that about one in every 10 elementary students suffers from a behavior disorder. The bad news is that the number is rising. It's important to be aware of the latest information on learning disabilities, Attention Deficit Disorder (ADD), Attention Deficit Hyperactivity Disorder (ADHD), and childhood depression. While the outlook may look overwhelming and even depressing, the good news is that God provides us the resources literally to save lives. The Gospel—the Good News of Jesus who came to earth to suffer and die on the cross for our sins—can and does transform troubled and challenged lives.

Of course, most children are not burdened by emotional or behavioral problems. Most preteens are happy and content with their lives. (That, of course, doesn't mean they will never complain.) They usually have an exuberance for living. They realize they are developing more independence and with it comes responsibility; most rise to the opportunity. They will sometimes experience mood swings and seem to jump from being confident to insecure, but just wait until the hormones really take off! They have begun the journey of finding themselves. This process will take them into the period of adolescence and beyond.

Eleven- and 12-year-olds view rules differently than the younger child. They realize that rules can be changed to fit the situation when the people involved agree to it. Some seem to delight in determining their own rules. At times, they need guidance in limiting the rules they make; it is not essential to have a rule for every situation that might be encountered. In deciding their own rules, they begin to understand the spirit of the law as well as the letter of the law. They realize that a person's intent can assist in determining guilt. When deciding punishment, they often feel the offender should suffer the same fate as the victim.

Most preteens are still in Erikson's period of Industry vs. Inferiority. They like keeping busy. When they fail they need reassurance that they can learn from mistakes. As they become more competitive, assist them in comparing their work to only their own previous work and not to another student's. Some have already begun the move into the stage of Identity vs. Role Confusion, in which finding one's identity becomes the most controlling factor of their life.

While most preteens are still in Fowler's stage 2 faith thinking (and a few probably in stage 1), some are beginning to think along stage 3 lines. In stage 2, stories are taken literally. Many fifth and sixth graders begin to understand some abstract symbols but only when they can connect them with something concrete. When symbols are used, teaching of the concrete must preface it.

Westerhoff would put most preteens at the transition between Experienced Faith and Affiliative Faith. Even when students make this transition earlier than their peers, one must remember that a person never outgrows her need for Experienced Faith. Affiliative Faith craves the feeling of belonging to a community. Preteens need to be involved in their community. Fifth and sixth graders love to acolyte for worship services. They often jump at the chance to assist in ushering. Boys as well as girls are comfortable singing publicly, because their voices have not yet begun to change. Some congregations commune fifth and sixth graders after instruction that includes both the child and his or her parents. This practice could strengthen their faith at a time when they may begin to question it, while it reinforces their feelings of belonging to their faith community.

In Gillespie's view, the preteen is about to make the move from Reflected Faith to Personalized Faith. Now is the time to build a strong foundation of knowledge in God's Word. They are old enough to serve their congregations in various capacities; allow them opportunities for this.

At this point in life, some students still appear to like memory work as it gives them a sense of accomplishment. They are often capable of memorizing lengthy selections. Now is a good time to promote memorization of Luther's Small Catechism since it gives a solid doctrinal foundation.

The prayers of preteens are less egocentric and materialistic than those of younger children, but they still expect a quick answer to prayer. Most will be able to identify that God answers prayers with a yes, no, or wait, but they have difficulty accepting a no or a wait response to their own lives. Those who come from a "praying" background will be able to pray extemporaneously; others prefer a printed prayer when it is their turn to lead the class in prayer.

Fifth and sixth graders like to talk about their faith and discuss issues that bother them. They are adept at listening to the opinions of others and peers can often answer their questions as clearly as the teacher is able. They want to know how to apply their faith to everyday situations. Although group discussion usually comes easily for them, they need activity-based application. Roleplaying and making comic strips are just two ways to achieve this.

This age can be challenging for teachers, but the rewards are worth it. Jesus will bless your efforts to guide and nurture preteens. You can help lay the foundation for a God-pleasing adolescence. You will see the work of the Spirit take hold as their peer relationships deepen and as they demonstrate their faith in the words and actions of everyday life. You'll praise God for using you in His plan when a blossoming 15-year-old just stops by to say hi! (Know that it means more than just hello.)

ACTIVITIES FOURTH GRADERS ENJOY

1. Play games like Bible scavenger hunt
2. Roleplay
3. Learn to use concordances
4. Write free verse poems about Bible characters
5. Write letters to Bible characters
6. Collect and display small items that remind them of God's blessings
7. Make dioramas of Bible stories
8. Use a prayer box
9. Design tracts
10. Make Bible storybooks for younger children
11. Design a Christian calendar of the church year
12. Plan and lead class devotions
13. Celebrate baptismal birthdays in a way that's not too childish
14. Make Bible story puppets; use them to teach the story to younger students
15. Design a bulletin board display
16. Make a Christian coat of arms
17. Make "stained-glass window" mosaics

ACTIVITIES FIFTH AND SIXTH GRADERS ENJOY

1. Roleplay
2. Design bulletin boards with a specific theme of your lesson
3. Learn to use a variety of reference materials
4. Create a timeline of Jesus' life
5. Participate in a Seder meal
6. Rewrite a parable as Jesus might have told it today
7. Adopt shut-ins
8. Send cards to sick members of the congregation
9. Write a letter to God thanking Him for an adult in their life
10. Make banners to be used in church (Baptism, confirmation, etc.)
11. Perform service projects such as mending hymnals or sharpening pew pencils
12. Make Christian message buttons
13. Pick a mission country to learn about and send money to missionaries there
14. Correspond with missionaries
15. Make murals of Bible stories
16. Make mobiles of the fruit of the Spirit
17. Solve puzzles
18. Create word search puzzles with names of Bible heroes
19. Write skits to illustrate Bible truths
20. Invite a college student preparing for full-time ministry to speak to the class
21. Prepare and present a chapel service
22. Take field trips connected to your religion curriculum
23. Write to Concordia Gospel Outreach at Box 201, St. Louis, MO 63166-0201 or call (314) 268-1363 for information on how you can pass along usable Gospel materials—Sunday school curriculum, Bibles, *My Devotions,* and other Christian literature.

Implications of Research for Elementary Students

Researcher	Theory	What Does This Mean?
Piaget	Concrete operational transitioning to formal operational	Can mentally solve problems from what has been experienced to abstract thinking, form hypotheses and mentally solve problems
Erikson	Industry vs. Inferiority moving to Identity vs. Role Confusion	Intellectual curiosity leads to production moving to concern over who they are becoming; provide activities that focus on student describing self
Kohlberg	Conventional Morality (an action is right if it impresses those in authority)	Use news items to discuss moral dilemmas students can relate to; ask "why" questions; change circumstances—would decision change?
Fowler	Mythic-Literal Faith beginning to move to Synthetic-Conventional Faith	Fairness becoming less important; growing understanding of symbolism; beliefs accepted because others believe; forgiveness and love important
Westerhoff	Experienced Faith expands to Affiliative Faith	Still need affective experiences; involvement in service and worship of congregation
Gillespie	Reflected Faith to Personalized Faith	Use Bible heroes and memorization moving to open discussion; peer ministry; use activities to build personal relationships

Faith of Middle School Students

*B*efore you read this chapter, review the Publisher's Preface. *As you design learning experiences, remember that you can provide the context for faith to begin and grow. Only God can provide the power for that growth.*

In this chapter we shall use the term *junior high* for youth about 13–15 years old. In many parts of the country schools for these youth are called *middle school.*

Tell a total stranger that you teach junior high kids, and you will receive compliments on your bravery or a look that conveys that you must be a fool. Thirteen- to 15-year-olds bring out a strong response in just about every adult who hears the words *junior high.* But make no mistake about it, many junior high teachers would never consider teaching another age. Perhaps because the age can be so frustrating, the rewards can be so worthwhile. Connect with a young adolescent, and you can feel her energy and enthusiasm for life surge through you. On the other hand, for a teacher who fails to make the connection, working with junior high students is as draining as the energy wasted by a 35-year-old refrigerator that makes a lot of noise and barely gets the job done.

Think of junior high students. What comes to mind? Peer pressure? Awkwardness? Moodiness? Self-centeredness? Fascination with appearance? Conformity? Cliques? Puberty? Whatever it is, it's not a pretty picture! Think back to your junior high years. What were the stresses you had to contend with? In what ways is life different for today's young teenager?

Let's take a look at a typical week in the lives of Dana and Traci, a couple of teens.

THE JUNIOR HIGH STUDENT

Dana has attended St. Paul's School since she was in kindergarten. Her P.E. class is composed of both seventh and eighth grade girls. For the physical abilities testing, her teacher has paired her with Traci. Dana and Traci are about the same size and have similar physical abilities. Beyond that the two are worlds apart.

Dana is in seventh grade. She works hard to maintain her good grades. Even though everyone tells her she's smart, she doesn't trust her intelligence. She works slowly and meticulously. She always checks her answers before she turns in her work just to be on the safe side. Her locker is neat and organized. She greets all the teachers, even the ones she never had. In P.E. class, she always dresses out, is always on time, and tries hard to follow the teacher's directions.

Traci is an eighth grader. This is her second year at St. Paul's. Her parents admit they are not particularly religious, but they thought a smaller environment would be good for their daughter. You can tell Traci enjoys dressing stylishly and that labels are important to her. She is a pretty girl who uses a moderate amount of makeup but nothing too outrageous.

When Miss Davis announced the partners for the physical ability tests, Traci rolled her eyes and whispered to her best friend Amber. They both turned and stared at Dana. Dana's eyes stung with tears, but she blinked them back. She knew some of the other girls laughed at her glasses and the clothes her 20-year-old sister wore when she was in seventh grade. She knew she was one of the few who didn't shave her legs. She also knew she could survive being partnered with Traci. Her mom had told her many times that what she thought of herself was more important than what other people thought. She usually believed that, but some days it was difficult to accept her mom's maxims.

When it came time for the 100 yard dash, Dana sprinted for all she was worth. Her time wasn't in the world record category, but she was pleased that she was faster than last year. Then she got ready to clock Traci's dash. Traci could be a good athlete when she wanted. The finish line bordered the field where the boys were playing softball. The gun sounded, and Traci got off to a good start. Suddenly her attention seemed to be diverted from the finish line to Kyle, who was playing third base. He turned and watched her run. Traci slowed down. Dana was not impressed by the time she listed. She showed the card to Traci who shrugged her shoulders and said, "Who wants to sweat?"

Dana's best friend moved away last summer. She doesn't hate going to school, but she's lonely. She sees Traci surrounded by the most popular boys and girls and doesn't quite understand why. From her perspective, Traci is not a particularly kind person. She only seems to care about herself or making fun of other people. It's not that Traci says lots of mean things, it's just the way she looks at her or how she laughs with her friends who all look away when Dana approaches them.

Dana is thankful that Traci is not on the volleyball team. She's also grateful that Mrs. Jenner, the third grade teacher, coaches the team. Mrs. Jenner knows how to help the team improve their skills, and she also cares about the players individually. Dana knows Mrs. Jenner will always have time to listen when she stops by her classroom. The only problem is that Mrs. Jenner is pregnant. Will she still be around after the baby is born?

Traci, on the other hand, is mystified by Dana. How can somebody not try to look her best and especially not shave her legs? Although she'd never admit it to her friends, Traci thinks Dana would be pretty if she fixed herself up a little. Smiling more would help, too. Traci has heard how smart Dana is. She wouldn't mind being a little smarter. Her parents are always on her case to get good grades. She's embarrassed to work hard and still fail. So Traci puts in minimal effort and gets minimal grades. When a low test paper is returned to her, she just shrugs her shoulders and flashes her cute smile at Kyle.

Dana loves religion class. She reads the Bible even when she doesn't have to. She would tell you that she prays to God often, and she knows He always listens, even when He answers no, which He sometimes does because He knows what's best for her. She feels a special closeness to God in church and participates fully in worship. She's looking forward to eighth grade confirmation and being able to receive Holy Communion. Some days she stops by the church office on her way home and helps the secretary stuff the bulletins or she dusts the pews. Dana isn't sure what she wants to do with her life, but she's confident that whatever it is, she'll serve God.

Traci was never really exposed to much Christianity except for going to church on Christmas and Easter when her family visited her grandmother. She is struggling to learn all of the memory work that is required of eighth graders. She is seriously considering being confirmed in May; after all, most of her friends will be. Since most of the material is new to her, she finds religion class fairly interesting; however, sometimes she feels like she doesn't have a clue what her classmates are talking about.

The parable of the workers in the vineyard (Matthew 20:1–16) confused Traci. The class read it aloud and discussed what they thought it meant. When Traci realized that the workers who put in 12 hours were paid the same as those who worked just one, she blurted out, "That's not fair!" When the teacher asked her to explain, she tried to put her feelings into words, "I thought God was a God of love. He should have loved the workers who were there all day more because they did more." Kyle raised his hand to answer her. "That's precisely the point. God is a God of love. He doesn't play favorites. He loves everyone equally. Jesus came to earth to suffer and die for all sinners." Traci felt really confused, but she was too embarrassed to say anything else.

WORKING WITH JUNIOR HIGH STUDENTS

At the beginning of seventh grade, some students are just 12 years old. By the end of eighth grade, some are already 15. The junior high student can be hard to categorize, because there's such a wide range to the norm. However, we will examine characteristics most young teens experience sooner or later.

Age alone will not determine which students reach physical maturity during this time and which will not. Heredity also plays a part. Some eighth grade boys will be large enough to play varsity football as a freshman; however, it's common for the smallest eighth grade student to be a boy. Girls generally hit their growth spurt earlier than boys, but by the eighth grade year many of the boys begin to catch up.

Along with the growth spurt come secondary sex characteristics. For girls that means the breasts develop, a waistline appears, the hips broaden, pubic hair grows, and oil-producing glands over-achieve. Boys experience a broadening of the shoulders, deepening of the voice, growth of pubic, facial, and body hair, and the oil-producing glands go into overdrive. On top of all of this, girls begin their menstrual cycle, and boys have wet dreams. And adults talk about stress!

Even when preteens know what to expect and are well-prepared for the assault of adolescence, this can be a period of uncertainty. Girls aren't sure if they're supposed to be proud of their blossoming figures or embarrassed. Sometimes that decision is determined by who notices the new shape. For many, this physical change compels a father—who is not sure how to react to the new woman in his life—into distancing himself from a daughter who needs him now more than ever. Boys tend to be proud of their new masculine traits, one of which includes "baby" fat turning into muscle tissue.

Late-arriving puberty can make a major impact on a teen's self-esteem. Males who mature in later adolescence might feel like they're a completely different species than their larger classmates. In physical competition, there's no contest. Answering questions in class, their voices squeak in contrast to the booming bass of the boy who sits behind them. A caring teacher makes sure all students feel valued and important in God's plan for them. Guide each student to finding his special place in school. One very effective junior high science teacher took several social outcasts under her wing and trained them to be her assistants. Most noon recesses found her little group rushing to help her set up for the next class or grading papers.

Just about all junior high students are concerned about their appearance. Most young teens would like the adults in their lives to believe they are the picture of self-confidence; however, almost all them are anxious about the way they appear to their peers. Compared to the images they see on television, they're not pretty enough, tall enough, slim enough, witty enough, athletic enough, masculine enough, etc., etc., etc. Notice that this trait isn't limited to girls. Families with teenagers will verify that as often as not it's their teenage son who's holed up in the bathroom trying to get his hair just right. Emotionally, this age is plagued by extreme mood swings. The 14-year-old feels his emotions much more strongly than the 8-year-old does, and it shows. The pendulum can swing from euphoria to despair with no warning. Often teens themselves cannot explain exactly what happened to make the emotions change so dramatically. At times they will act very adult, and the next day childishness prevails.

For most junior high students, one's peers have become the authority in determining behavior. Although this is difficult for many parents to accept, it is necessary for teens to make this move toward independence. Because the teen no longer looks to parents for primary approval, conforming to the dictates of the latest fad becomes important. This isn't limited to clothing or hair styles. Many a class discussion has been thwarted because few want to take a minority position. It sometimes helps to have students write their opinions of a topic and then read these to the class without identifying the writer.

Young adolescents are greatly concerned with what their peers think of them. Friends are one of the most important parts of their lives. Everyone needs a group to which to belong, a group that will give them an identity. Clubs, sports teams, and youth groups can all have a positive effect on teens. On the negative side, some find involvement with street gangs as a way to achieve identity. Not having a group of one's own can be devastating. Some are willing to commit petty crimes or experiment with drugs or sex to become part of a group.

Physical, emotional, and social changes aren't the only transformation young teens have to deal with. Most are in the process of moving from concrete operational thought to formal thought. They can hypothesize and mentally perform functions. They can grasp complex concepts and abstractions. However, this transition does not happen quickly. Students who sometimes use formal thought don't always think that way. Not all individuals achieve this ability at the same time. Students with higher level thinking skills might get very irritated at classmates who "just don't get it" through no fault of their own.

Adolescents need to be active physically as well as mentally. They need an outlet for their energy, which allows them to release tension. They like *doing* things, not just talking about them. Because of their strenuous activity combined with many physical changes brought about by rapid growth, they also need more sleep than they used to. Unfortunately, this occurs at the same time they think they ought to be allowed to determine their own bedtime or stay up later to watch television. They also have a tendency to be continually hungry. Good nutrition is essential. Girls think they ought to watch their weight. They often turn down nutritious meals and end up stuffing themselves with junk food instead. They need to hear and experience how a balanced diet benefits them. Teachers need to be aware that it's not too early for eating disorders to emerge.

Seventh and eighth grade students need to be noticed by their peers and the adults in their lives. Teachers provide feedback on their strengths and weaknesses, which can provide direction on future occupational goals. Whether the student is a class leader or extremely shy, every one needs a teacher who makes small talk with him or compliments a new dress or hair style. When Christian teachers convey that each student is important, they reinforce how significant every individual is in God's eyes.

Young teens need to be independent. They are beginning to distance themselves from their homes and families. This is a necessary step, but it can be painful for all involved. It actually takes a lot of courage to be critical of one's parents. That can cause guilt and anxiety in the teen, which adds more friction to the home. These teens tend to compare their parents to everybody else's parents; their parents always lose. They are sometimes embarrassed by their families' material possessions (or lack of them) compared to those of their friends. They want to do things on their own, in their own time, and in their own way. The wise teacher provides opportunities for students to make both personal and group decisions that help determine the direction the class takes.

Seventh and eighth graders need be loved and valued. They need to know that they are important to adults (even though they often communicate that adults are not real important to them). An empathetic teacher lets them know that their importance doesn't depend on their achievements or abilities. Jesus died for all of us while we were yet sinners. That means we don't have to earn God's love; we have it because of His goodness, not our actions. God loves us enough to say no when a yes would endanger us. God loves us enough to tell us in His Word what He expects of us. God loves us with a love that allows us to suffer natural consequences. When teachers love with God's unconditional love, students know they have value.

Adolescents need opportunities to show their love for God by loving others. Encountering new situations through service opportunities can be threatening and cause teens to be anxious; serving others with a group of peers makes it less intimidating. Congregations and schools can provide experiences to interact with preschoolers, do yard work for the elderly, or assist at soup kitchens. Many teens discover they enjoy helping others and continue their service activities throughout their lives.

Teens have a need to believe in something larger than themselves. This guides them on their search for identity. If we hope to nurture our youth for greater spiritual maturity, they must experience Christian adults who actively live their faith. We need to give them opportunities to express their faith. We need to listen and honestly answer their questions. We need to challenge them to live their faith in a hostile world. We need to share our successes and failures and always, always, always let them know how God uses us in spite of ourselves.

When we examine the theories of spiritual growth, experts all agree that early adolescence often brings a transition in the way individuals think about their faith. In Fowler's stage 3 faith, symbolism is used and understood. Teenagers typically conform to the attitudes and behavior of their peers. People with stage 3 faith strongly identify with those who are important to them. Teens in Christian settings often grow closer to God as God's Word comes to them through Christian friends and parents. They do not analyze why they believe as they do; they come to believe as those around them do. Relationships are critical in stage 3 faith. This can be their relationship with God or their relationships with fellow believers. The perceptive teacher uses many relationship-building activities.

Most junior high students would fall into Westerhoff's Affiliative Faith, which is marked by a strong sense of belonging to a community. Building a community spirit and identity is important in this style of faith. Don't forget that Experienced Faith is still part of the individual's life. A few of the more mature junior high students might be making the transition into Searching Faith, but this occurs more commonly in high school.

Personalized Faith begins in early adolescence, according to Gillespie's beliefs. Youth need the freedom to discuss issues that are important to them and to evaluate how their faith relates to these issues. Teens need a personalized, meaningful faith. Anything less is worthless in their eyes. Gillespie proposes that congregations find meaningful ways for youth to be involved.

If you want to make a difference in the lives of your junior high students, be sure they know they are loved and respected. They will test your love to be sure, but they want to know that love is genuine, can be trusted, and is unconditional. When they express defiant or hurtful behavior, you must deal with it. Ignoring the behavior does not show love to the student. Love can be communicated even when there are consequences to pay for choosing to disregard rules. Students respect adults who follow through with what is promised and who avoid making idle threats. When teachers treat students with courtesy and respect, they learn to respect themselves and each other. Learning can thrive in such an environment.

Teenagers can spot a phony a mile away. Don't try to be something you're not with them. Being yourself and letting your love for the Lord shine through your actions is the most effective religion lesson you can teach.

ACTIVITIES FOR JUNIOR HIGH STUDENTS

1. Construct classroom bulletin boards
2. Plan and conduct worship experiences
3. Tutor younger children
4. Count the offering
5. Write articles or develop comic strips for the Sunday school newspaper
6. Prepare newsletters or church bulletins
7. Tell a Bible story to a group of small children, using graphics of their own construction
8. Develop, produce, and distribute their own greeting cards to the sick or lonely
9. Accompany a pastor on a sick call
10. Write a commercial for salvation
11. Use the jingles of current commercials to explain the attributes of God
12. Write similes and metaphors to describe God
13. Write modern parables explaining salvation or forgiveness
14. Roleplay opportunities to apply Law and Gospel in real-life situations
15. Illustrate your concept of the Last Day
16. Write thank-you notes to people who have impacted your faith life; mail them
17. Make banners of the church year
18. Create and present a chancel drama
19. Roleplay peer problems and possible solutions
20. Prepare and present skits about the relationships between parents and their teenagers
21. Listen to and discuss popular songs
22. Invite a guest speaker from the Fellowship of Christian Athletes to speak to the class
23. Plan, prepare, and show a video production
24. Make collages that tell about you
25. Interview your parents to find out what their lives were like when they were your age

Implications of Research for Junior High/Middle School Students

Researcher	Theory	What Does This Mean?
Piaget	Formal operational (can deal with abstract concepts, form hypotheses, solve problems systematically, use mental manipulation	Teens assume others think as they do about themselves; begin lesson with concrete ideas, then move to more abstract; discuss symbolism
Erikson	Identity vs. Role Confusion (teens seek to establish an identity)	Teens are confused about what behaviors will be accepted by others; create climate of acceptance and recognition
Kohlberg	Conventional Morality: Good boy/nice girl orientation (the right action impresses others)	Discuss moral issues; teach communication skills; teach acceptance
Fowler	Synthetic-Conventional Faith (believing what the church believes)	Teens want a God who knows, understands, and accepts them; need a strong sense of community
Westerhoff	Affiliative Faith (one's community gives identity)	Teens need to be involved in church activities; connect head knowledge with heart knowledge
Gillespie	Personalized Faith (finding a faith to own)	Teens need open discussion, involvement, peer ministry

Chapter 9

Faith of High School Students

*B*efore you read this chapter, review the Publisher's Preface. *As you design learning experiences, remember that you can provide the context for faith to begin and grow. Only God can provide the power for that growth.*

As I neared the completion of this book, my 17-year-old daughter came into the room and asked me how it was going. I told her I was almost done with only one more chapter to write. "What's that one on?" she asked. When I responded that it would be on high school students, she loudly announced, "Don't categorize us. Don't try to generalize us. There is no normal! Everything is accepted. We are!" I suppose she about summed it up.

Mention of the high school student evokes a strong response in many adults. For some, the response is anger. "They're lazy and afraid of hard work. All you ever see are kids hanging around and getting in trouble. They're rude and obnoxious." For others, the response is confusion. "Why do they dress that way? Why would any boy want to shave his head/wear a mohawk/wear a ponytail? Why do they listen to that music? Why don't they come to church after they're confirmed?" High school teens intimidate some. "Go to the mall or out for fast food, and they're all you see. You'd think they own the place. Don't they have any morals? They hang all over each other. The streets aren't safe with the way they drive. I just wish they'd go away."

Teaching high school students involves challenges. Ideally, people with the attitudes mentioned above won't be working with this age group. However, probably most high school teachers have experienced at least one of those emotional responses at one time or another. High schoolers can be confusing at times. After all, they will usually admit they're confused on many issues. They can be intimidating. They know it and know when they can use intimidation to their advantage. They can make an adult angry. After all, some reason, if we get angry at ourselves, we should be entitled to make others feel the same way.

What does it mean to be a high school student in today's society? What challenges and pressures do they have to deal with? What are their joys? What sorrows confront them? Or was my daughter right? Is it impossible to generalize about teenagers? What if there is no norm?

One thing is certain. Every teen is an individual and has a unique personality. Yet teenagers share common concerns. There are developmental tasks that they need to achieve in order to move into mature adulthood. Let's take a look.

THE HIGH SCHOOL STUDENT

The Bailey household is seldom calm and quiet. They have two teenagers. Larissa is 15 and in ninth grade; Jon is an 18-year-old senior. They live with both parents and two dogs.

Jon is active in his Christian high school. He is a distance runner on the cross-country and track teams. He has played saxophone in the band for four years. He doesn't hang around the most popular group in school, but that doesn't bother him. In addition to his other activities, he is the sound technician for the school's premier singing group that travels to area churches for monthly performances. Most of his closest friends are part of this group. The director, Mr. Eggers or "Mr. E," is young and personable. He relates well to teens, and Jon counts him as a friend.

Larissa is beginning to run as well. She wasn't sure she wanted to join the team, but the coach hounded her until she finally showed up for practice. She also plays in the school band but has made it perfectly clear that hers is only a one-year stint. Once her fine arts elective is satisfied, she is giving it up. While most of Jon's friends are on the running team or connected with music, Larissa still spends most of her time with friends from elementary school—although she's getting to know a lot more people this year.

Jon is busy with college applications and searching for scholarships. He has wanted to be involved with the outdoors since he was 12; now he's hoping for a career in environmental biology. He's looking forward to moving out of state for college. He has a girlfriend, but they're not particularly serious. They enjoy each other's company and have a lot of mutual friends. They plan to keep in touch during college, but by mutual agreement they've agreed that it's okay to date other people.

Larissa doesn't really know what she wants to do with her life, except that she definitely does not want to be a teacher like her mother. She likes science but states that she's tired of following in her brother's footsteps. She wants to do something totally different than what he does. She doesn't have a boyfriend, although there's a boy in her Spanish class that she'd like to get to know better. He acts like he's interested, too. She is afraid that if he asks her out, her parents will say she's too young to date.

Jon is a serious student. He usually spends three or four hours a night on homework. He knows he is a perfectionist, but that doesn't stop him from working harder than most of his friends. He rationalizes that they are smarter, and he has to work that much harder to get the grades they get.

Larissa is also a good student, but she only spends an hour or two on homework a night. Her parents are not surprised by this. She's taking the same college prep classes that Jon took, with mostly the same teachers; yet with a lot less effort, she's getting the same good grades he earned. Her parents had always been pleased with their son's academic work ethic, but now they're wondering if he couldn't be a little more like her. While Jon is slaving away to ensure he has his work exactly right, Larissa is talking on the phone or watching TV, knowing that the rest of her evening is free.

Both Jon and Larissa have a pretty good relationship with their parents. Some of Jon's friends kid him about his "perfect family." The Baileys take camping vacations every summer and worship together almost every week. Eating dinner together is the rule, not the exception. Both parents try to get to as many of the kids' track and cross-country meets as possible.

Mr. and Mrs. Bailey were both raised as Christians. They are regular in their worship but not as involved in their large congregation as they know they ought to be. Both Jon and Larissa participate in the church youth group activities, although Larissa will first conduct a telephone poll to find out which of her friends will be attending. Jon occasionally attends the Sunday night youth service at his girlfriend's nondenominational Christian church. At first he thought his parents would object to this, but they are grateful he's dating a Christian girl who seems to take her faith seriously.

Like any other brother and sister, Jon and Larissa have their bad moments. They share the upstairs bathroom and can seldom agree on who gets it when. They still argue about who gets to dry the dishes and who has to wash them. But as much as they sometimes disagree, they are really very close. When Larissa needs advice, she's as likely to go to her brother as to her parents. At the beginning of the year Jon moaned about having his little sister at the same high school, but now he actually watches out for her. He's not sure how he'd react if one of his friends asked her out. Almost every night the two spend about 15 minutes in a mock battle that starts over some inconsequential disagreement and escalates into a wrestling match.

Jon is looking forward to moving to college. His parents agree— they will miss him, but it's time for him to go. There's probably more conflict between Larissa and her mom than anyone else. Larissa accuses her mother of wanting her to be just like Jon. Her mother can't figure out what she says to give Larissa that impression. She just wants her daughter to make wise choices in life.

WORKING WITH HIGH SCHOOL STUDENTS

Working with high schoolers is an exciting opportunity. They are almost, but not quite, adults. The door to their future is right in front of them. In some respects they are very much like their grandparents were when they were teenagers, and yet their world is totally different. Friction and conflict have existed between parents and teens since Cain and Abel hit adolescence, but within the course of just a few years, many will say that their parents have been the most influential people in their lives.

Fifteen- to 18-year-olds usually attain physical maturity and practically all have hit puberty. By the time of high school graduation, most teens have finished growing, although some boys will continue to grow into their early 20s. Concern about appearance is not as important to most students as it was in junior high. Acne is still a cause for distress. For boys especially, the sex drive is more pronounced than ever before.

High school students tend to fall in Erikson's stage of Identity vs. Role Confusion. Probably youth's most important developmental task is to determine who and what they will be. Throughout their childhood their parents have given them strong messages that tell them who they are. Their value system and behavior have in a large part been bestowed by their parents. At this point in their lives, teens determine how much of that parent-given identity they want to retain and what they will reject. They usually decide to take some ideas from their peers for their own. They sample values and discard those that don't work for them. Whether they realize it or not, they are defining the direction the remainder of their lives will most likely take.

For most, the biggest roadblock to gaining identity is confusion about sexual and occupational identity. In personality development the term *identity* relates to a sense of personal well-being. Teens who suffer from role confusion have trouble deciding what behaviors will receive a favorable reaction from others. They do not have a sense of knowing where they are headed in life, and they experience disequilibrium.

In the area of sexual identity, confusion results when youth must choose between the values adult authorities and the church cherish and those offered by the world and their own sex drive. Hormones can speak louder than words. Studies have determined that in teenage boys production of testosterone can increase tenfold within a six-month period. Girls are more likely to have premarital intercourse if their girlfriends are involved in a sexual relationship. For girls there is also a correlation between grades and sexual activity. On one hand, parents, church, and school warn of the dangers of sexual involvement. On the other, movies, music, peers, and one's own body suggest that to abstain is to miss out. When you're in the middle of this tug-of-war, life feels frayed, no matter what your decision. Adding to the bewilderment for some, society seems to now accept homosexuality as a lifestyle option. For individuals still trying to figure out their sexual feelings, this compounds the confusion.

Today's teens grapple with the issues of teenage pregnancy (just as their parents and grandparents did, although the rates are rising) and sexually transmitted diseases (a problem more talked about now than in the past). This doesn't mean to imply that these are problems they deal with on a firsthand basis; they are issues teens care about. Some students are faced with helping friends who are facing these problems. They find no easy answers. Parents, schools, and the church must be open to talk about these issues and listen to what teens have to say. Open communication is only one step, but perhaps it's the most important step toward curbing runaway sexuality.

In our present society the changing sex roles for men and women complicate the problems teens face. No longer are women expected to be solely wife and mother; now females are often expected to be co-breadwinners. Teenage girls are already discussing whether they want to have an established career before they start a family or have their children and then try to "make it" in their chosen profession.

Modern technology, which constantly replaces itself, is perpetually changing the design of the workplace. People are flocking to jobs that didn't exist a generation ago. New, necessary positions are opening all the time. How does one plan for a place in a future world that will doubtless have many technical breakthroughs before you get there? What if you train for a job that is no longer necessary by the time you're ready to join the work force? One's occupational choices will determine much of one's future—how time is spent, earning power, and where and how one lives. No wonder teens often panic at the thought of making a career commitment.

Peer acceptance is essential for the teenager; it appears to be a stronger concern for girls than boys. Boys tend to base friendship on common interests and abilities, such as sports or recreation. Bonding is more important to girls. Because of this, girls tend to worry about friends; they sometimes feel threatened when a close friend makes a new friend. Many girls would say that friends are the most important part of their lives.

Peers definitely influence the behavior of teenagers. To some extent almost every teen dresses like her peers and wears a hairstyle accepted by her peers. Friends are often determined by peers. Peers shape dating patterns, recreation, and the hours an individual keeps. Even eating habits can be molded by one's peers.

Parents are often concerned that peers have too much influence in their teenager's life. Probably no family with teens has escaped an argument centering on wanting to do what one's friends do. When it comes to decisions teens make that affect the present (clothing, recreation, choice of friends), peers do have a strong influence. However, studies have shown that parents have a greater influence on decisions that affect the long run, such as choice of career or religious beliefs and values.

Mood swings are common in high school students. To paraphrase a famous author, adolescence is both the best time of life and the worst time of life. When life is treating the teenager well, she's sitting on top of the world. Her friends are there for her, grades may not be great, but at least she's getting what she expected, the opposite sex is paying attention, and no adults have been on her case. During times like these she's energetic and outgoing. Sometimes when one thing goes wrong, it appears (to her) that everything is headed downhill. A broken date, a low test grade, a cutting remark by a teacher, a disagreement with a friend, or not achieving a personal goal can all trigger dismay. To the teen it seems as if their world is falling apart, and no one cares.

Many students experience depression at one time or another or stand by a friend who is dealing with this emotional disorder. Depression is often caused by a sense of loss connected to the feeling that one has no control over his life. The loss might be breaking up with a girlfriend, failure to make the team, a serious accident or illness, or death of a loved one. Sometimes eating disorders appear (more common in females than males), drugs are abused, or thoughts of suicide seem to dominate his thoughts. Anyone working with teens needs to be aware that threats of suicide need to be taken seriously. Talking about committing suicide is a call for help.

In the cognitive domain, most high schoolers are capable of using formal thought. They can mentally plan a process for achieving a goal, test a hypothesis in a logical manner, and understand abstract relationships. Of course, just because they can do these things doesn't mean that they will always use more advanced thinking skills. Sometimes they need to be encouraged to do so; a high school teacher needs to begin with concrete examples and then move to more abstract ideas. Some students might be overwhelmed by the number of possibilities they can imagine as a solution to a problem. These individuals need guidance to look for practical, realistic answers in their discussions of problems.

In the field of moral development, Kohlberg places teenagers in the stage of Conventional Morality, with many high school students having a law and order orientation. With this type of reasoning, one would obey laws because they are the glue that holds society together. Authority needs to be respected; otherwise, chaos would result.

In the process of faith development, Fowler puts most high school students in stage 3 faith, Synthetic-Conventional Faith. Teens want to identify with a group. Their group's beliefs and values become their own. If this group is church based, they usually stay active in worship and other church-related activities. If their group has no use for religion, the teen will probably reject religion as well, at least temporarily. Teens are looking for acceptance and affirmation from their friends. They want no less from God and their church. At this age they are more than aware of their own sinfulness and inadequacies. The concept of a loving, forgiving God is very appealing.

Not all teenagers will be in stage 3 faith. This is especially evident when a teen has recently come to faith. For those growing up in a home characterized more by distrust than trust, the acceptance of God's love can be especially challenging. In a few cases, building a trust relationship with a teacher might be a first experience in understanding what trust is all about and exactly what the concepts of love, forgiveness, grace, and mercy mean. A teacher must listen carefully to what every student says about God and how he relates to the attributes of God. Teachers also need to consider what students don't say.

In Westerhoff's perception of faith development, most high schoolers would be in Affiliative Faith, with some moving into Searching Faith. In Affiliative Faith, the teen wants to be a part of the group. Heart knowledge, the affective realm of life, is most important. Learning the authority, or how actions are judged right or wrong, is meaningful. As pointed out earlier, Experienced Faith, the first style of faith, is still a part of the person and needs to be provided for also.

As teens move into the next style, Searching Faith, they are moving toward spiritual maturity, even though it might appear they have lost their faith. They are looking for personal meaning, and sometimes it seems they are looking for it everywhere but the church. The process of a Searching Faith involves experimentation.

Church bodies often have trouble supporting people at this stage in their life, but support and understanding is crucial if we don't want to drive the older adolescent away. The searching individual still needs to be included in the faith community; he still needs to feel wanted and valued.

Gillespie believes that high school brings a transition from Personalized Faith to Established Faith. To have an established faith, one must first question her personalized faith. Some aspects of her previous experience of faith will be discarded, and she will move on to new ideas and beliefs that make sense to her way of thinking. Discussion of theology and what God says about the issues she faces are important to her. Open communication is essential. If Jesus is the Word, the organized church cannot be afraid of words. Working through this process of discovering God's stand on the issues motivates her to "put her money where her mouth is" when it comes to her faith. The church must foster an environment where this can happen.

So what can a teacher do to guide teenagers to spiritual maturity? First, a climate of trust and respect needs to be established. Perhaps adolescence is just as critical as infancy for establishing trust. Without trust one cannot build a positive relationship between teacher and student. Without a positive relationship, a teacher will have little influence on a youth's faith. The teacher must trust the students and respect them as individuals. She needs to create an environment where the students are safe in trusting each other.

Respecting the students implies that the teacher understands that each person is unique. The teacher takes the time necessary to get to know each student personally. She looks them in the eye and listens to what they have to say. She cares about them as individuals and communicates her care. When this is done, she will earn their respect. Respect can't be demanded or bought. Don't expect high school students to respect you just because you're the teacher. Earn it. Don't expect to be their peer. Be the caring adult in charge (even when you're closer to their age than you might like to admit).

High school students need to be affirmed. They need to know we value them because they're the people they are, not because they have achieved special honors or accomplished a particular task. Affirmations can let the students know that the trials they face are not easy, but that they are a necessary part of growing up. Affirmations can remind the adult that students are in process and not yet at the end of their journey. Affirming actions include changing plans when necessary, paying attention to the individual, and being interested in students' welfare beyond the classroom.

Teens need teachers with good listening and speaking skills. Listening allows time for people to think. Some students are reflective thinkers; they will not respond to any question quickly. The silence might be deafening at first, but soon the group will expect time to consider a response. When answers are shared, be sure to check if you understood their position correctly. Students will appreciate that you care enough about their viewpoints to check for proper understanding.

If you expect the students to be honest with you, you must be honest with them. I once knew a pastor who wanted to do youth ministry, but he wasn't willing to share his shoe size in a get-acquainted game. Be willing to share your feelings and experiences. At times you will not be comfortable answering a question. If you can say, "That makes me uncomfortable. I feel like I can't win no matter how I respond," they will appreciate your honesty—as long as you don't use those words too frequently.

Teenagers need to interact with one another. Provide activities where they can share ideas and laughter. Always keeping teens in one large group can inhibit interaction; occasionally split into small groups or have students work with partners. Teens often have to be trained how to act in an environment of trust. Let them know your ground rules. "No put downs. Listen to others' opinions before you react." Give teens opportunities to share past experiences, current feelings, and plans for the future. Let them know it's safe to be honest because they will be accepted where they're at.

Teenagers need to be a part of their church's ministry, not just a presence that implies the congregation has a future. Just as adult members of a congregation have a variety of gifts and an assortment of ways they're involved in the local parish, teens don't want to be pigeonholed into one or two areas of involvement. Do youth have a voice in how the congregation is governed? Do they have voting privileges or at least speaking rights at voters meetings? May they teach or assist in Sunday school classes or vacation Bible school? What about ushering? When they're included in the total ministry of the church, teens stay involved in congregational life.

Does teaching high school students in an effort to help them grow to spiritual maturity sound like a massive job? It isn't. It's a job in which the Holy Spirit promises you assistance and counsel. It's one where the most important thing you can do is be yourself and live/model your faith.

ACTIVITIES TO INVOLVE HIGH SCHOOL STUDENTS

1. Have representatives on various church boards
2. Teach or assist with classes of younger students
3. Visit shut-ins
4. Participate in drama ministry
5. Serve as ushers
6. Participate in a youth branch of congregation's prayer chain
7. Serve at congregational dinners
8. Lead youth Bible studies
9. Work in the church nursery
10. Assist in worship
11. Sing in the choir or play in the band
12. Assist in the church office
13. Read the lessons in church
14. Organize and publicize youth events
15. Have offering envelopes
16. Coach younger students
17. Participate in voters meetings
18. Attend retreats and youth gatherings
19. Greet church visitors
20. Write articles for the church newsletter

Implications of Research for High School Students

Researcher	Theory	What Does This Mean?
Piaget	Formal operational (can deal with abstract concepts, form hypotheses, solve problems systematically, use mental manipulation)	Teens still need to connect concrete with abstract ideas; enjoy symbolism; sometimes get carried away with possible solutions
Erikson	Identity vs. Role Confusion (teens seek to establish an identity)	Confusion about sex and occupational roles; need discussion, affirmation from adults
Kohlberg	Conventional Morality: Law and Order Orientation (rules hold society together)	Discuss moral issues affecting today's teens; teach acceptance and communication skills
Fowler	Synthetic-Conventional Faith (believing what the church believes)	Teens need acceptance and affirmation; build sense of community
Westerhoff	Affiliative to Searching Faith (identity comes from community to search for personal meaning)	Create a climate that accepts questions and isn't threatened by looking at other faith traditions
Gillespie	Personalized Faith to Established Faith (finding a faith of one's own to examining that faith to work for the individual)	Open communication and discussion; challenge to live faith in daily lives

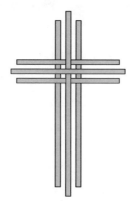

For Further Reading

*T*hese books may help the reader gain a greater understanding of the various learning and faith development theories. Concordia Publishing House, however, does not necessarily support each author's theological point of view.

Droege, Thomas A. *Faith Passages and Patterns.* Philadelphia: Fortress Press, 1983.

Dykstra, Craig, and Parks, Sharon, eds. *Faith Development and Fowler.* Birmingham, Alabama: Religious Education Press, 1986.

Fowler, James W. *Stages of Faith: The Psychology of Human Development and the Quest for Meaning.* San Francisco: Harper & Row, 1981.

Fowler, James W.; Nipkow, Karl Ernst; and Schweitzer, eds. *Stages of Faith and Religious Development: Implications for Church, Education, and Society.* New York: The Crossroad Publishing Company, 1991.

Gillespie, V. Bailey. *The Experience of Faith.* Birmingham, Alabama: Religious Education Press, 1988.

Morgenthaler, Shirley K. *Right from the Start: A New Parent's Guide to Child Faith Development.* St. Louis: Concordia Publishing House, 1989.

Moser, Carl J., and Schmidt, Arnold E., eds. *Integrating the Faith: A Teacher's Guide for Curriculum in Lutheran Schools.* St. Louis: Concordia Publishing House, 1986.

Niemi, Susan R.; Schmidt, Arnold; and Einess, Holly, eds. *Teaching the Faith* (series). Minneapolis: Augsburg Fortress and St. Louis: Concordia Publishing House, 1993.

Stokes, Kenneth. *Faith Is a Verb: Dynamics of Adult Faith Development.* Mystic, Connecticut: Twenty-third Publications, 1989.

Westerhoff, John H., III. *Will Our Children Have Faith?* San Francisco: Harper & Row, 1976.

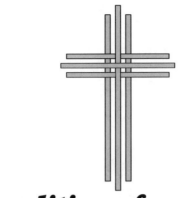

Conditions for Credit

1. No fewer than six 60-minute class sessions shall be held.
2. Attendance at 75 percent of the class sessions shall be required.
3. At least one hour of preparation shall be requested of all students in advance of each of the class sessions.
4. The textbooks and instructor's guides recommended by the Department of Child Ministry, 1333 S. Kirkwood Road, St. Louis, MO 63122-7295, shall be used.
5. An instructor other than the pastor ought to be approved by the local pastor in order to obtain credit for students. This approval shall be indicated by the pastor's signature on the application blank for credit.
6. The application for credit should be sent to the Department of Child Ministry immediately after the completion of the course.